MEAN

Also from Emily Books

The Gift by Barbara Browning
I'll Tell You in Person by Chloe Caldwell
Problems by Jade Sharma

MEAN

Myriam Gurba

COFFEE HOUSE PRESS
An Emily Books Original
Minneapolis and Brooklyn
2017

Coffee House Press books are available to the trade through our primary distributor, Consortium Book Sales & Distribution, cbsd.com or (800) 283-3572. For personal orders, catalogs, or other information, write to info@coffeehousepress.org.

Coffee House Press is a nonprofit literary publishing house. Support from private foundations, corporate giving programs, government programs, and generous individuals helps make the publication of our books possible. We gratefully acknowledge their support in detail in the back of this book.

LIBRARY OF CONGRESS CATALOGING-IN-PUBLICATION DATA

Names: Gurba, Myriam, author.
Title: Mean / Myriam Gurba.
Description: Minneapolis : Coffee House Press, 2017.
Identifiers: LCCN 2017012422 | ISBN 9781566894913 (softcover)
Subjects: LCSH: Gurba, Myriam. | Mexican American women authors—21st century—Biography. | Mexican American lesbians—Biography. | BISAC: BIOGRAPHY & AUTOBIOGRAPHY / Personal Memoirs. | BIOGRAPHY & AUTOBIOGRAPHY / Women. | BIOGRAPHY & AUTOBIOGRAPHY / Literary.
Classification: LCC PS3607.U5485 Z46 2017 | DDC 813/.6 [B]—dc23
LC record available at https://lccn.loc.gov/2017012422

ACKNOWLEDGMENTS

Thanks to the philosophers, poets, artists, and weirdos who influenced and populate this book. Hugs to Ruth and Emily for paying attention to my words. Kisses to Bob and Beatriz for giving me language and a family. Hugs and kisses to my guayabas on this planet and beyond. Thanks to Terri and Kalani for letting me edit at their henpecked dining room table. Thanks to Tiombe for helping me sort out my "issues." Thanks to RADAR Productions for supporting queer writing, art, performance, and me. Thanks to the cowboy for his Slavic generosity. Thanks to Lee for putting up with my shit. Thanks to the drama teacher for the love and drama. Thanks to Wendy for being a good Taurus sister. Thanks to David and Yasmin. Thanks to the ghosts.

PRINTED IN THE UNITED STATES OF AMERICA

24 23 22 21 20 19 18 17   1 2 3 4 5 6 7 8

For the restless.
But not the young.

"Lo mejor que te puedo desear es que te vaya mal."

—JENNI RIVERA

Contents

MEAN

Wisdom

Let's become a spot upon which fateful moonlight shines.

Let's become that night.

Let's become that park.

Let's absorb and drip. We're damp grains of earth. We're grass purged of color. We're baseball bleachers. We're November's darkness. We're the baseball diamond's sediment. We host Little League games by daylight. By dark, we become an Aztec altar.

We open our eyes. We allow them to adjust to the place and things described.

Seasonal quiet prevails.

Nothing squeaks or whimpers.

Nothing hums.

In a tunnel beneath the bleachers, a gopher daydreams. Roots sigh. Earthworms blindly go about their business.

A dark-haired girl walks alone.

Her foot falls onto the grass. We see up her skirt. She's not wearing underwear, so we can see that special part of her. It's the hole Persephone fell into. Some swine fell down it too.

Her clothes are long. Her dark-blue jacket sweeps her knees.

She slouches. She walks as if in mourning.

She steps into the outfield.

She pauses.

"Who's there?" she calls out in Spanish.

Silence responds.

She clutches her white purse. Her fingers worry its strap.

She nears the pitcher's mound, walks across it, heads toward home, and walks across it too. She crouches and climbs through a gash torn into the chain-link backstop.

She reaches into her purse. Mexican hair falls across her face.

It won't look like that much longer.

A man wearing white clothes creeps around the corner of the snack bar. He creeps up behind the girl and swings a pipe. It hits her in the head and her knees buckle. The man raises his weapon, takes another swing, and whacks her again.

He reaches down his sweatpants. He fondles his penis.

At sunset, a vendor in a straw cowboy hat had pushed his cart along the sidewalk yards away. Making his way down Western Avenue, the vendor had shouted, "¡Elote! ¡Elote! ¡Elote con mantequilla! ¡Elote con mayonesa!"

The man had heard these calls for corn.

He bought none.

Lovingly, he strokes his corn. It quivers. He lets go of it and resumes his chase.

She scrambles up the bleachers, panting. She bleeds onto benches. Blood on concrete. She hears him coming. She lurches, her purse tips, and two receipts sail. A nail file spills. Her toothbrush hits the ground bristles first. She scrambles further along the bench. She slips and falls. Her weight smashes against her elbow.

She crawls. Wet palm prints lengthen behind her. Blood smears her clothes. It makes dark Rorschachs on various surfaces.

Hard-packed dirt rubs her knees.

The man in white stands beside her. Blood dapples his T-shirt.

He kicks her. She flips onto her back. He slides a knife out of his pocket, takes a step, and stands so that he straddles her waist. He lowers himself onto her chest, squats, and leans toward her face. He presses his blade to her skin and slides it along her cheekbone. Black oozes from the slit. Wrecking her makes him feel like she belongs to him. We may feel that because we are privy to the wreckage she belongs to us too, but she does not.

He pushes her legs apart. He pulls out his corn and kneels. Blood pours from her cheek, nose, and head as he feeds himself into her. He thrusts to the rhythm of her death rattle. Her agony sustains his erection, holding it.

He freezes. He moans and shivers. His slack corn slides out of her. Cum oozes from between her legs. It gleams like unspeakable poetry.

// //

A newscaster described the murder as "the bludgeoning death of a transient in Oakley Park."

This description is cruel. It reduces her to transience, as if she personified it, and it ignores her name. Her name matters. It's a word that philosophers fall in love with.

It appears many times in the Bible: Sophia. In Greek, *sophia* means *wisdom.*

I turn her name over and over in my head. My brain rubs it smooth from *S* to *a.*

Sophia.

In my grim reverie, I think, "She's the capital of Bulgaria. I love Bulgarian yogurt. So rich, so tart, so *mean.* So grown up."

My mind keeps rubbing her name. An hourglass fills my imagination: Sophia Loren.

I light a votive candle, watch the flame bounce, and whisper her name aloud.

It sounds like breath. Transient sibilance runs through it.

// //

Sophia is always with me. She haunts me.

Guilt is a ghost.

// //

Sometimes, in my car, I realize I've been listening to Mexican music I'm not really into. A ranchera will be blaring, a man with a nasal voice will be moaning lyrics about heartache, and an accordion will join him.

I think, "Why am I listening to this? I don't even *like* this." Then I'll remember: *Sophia* . . .

// //

Some ghosts listen to the radio through the bodies of the living. They use us to conduct pain, pleasure, music, and meaning. They burden us with feelings that are both ours and theirs.

English Is Spanish

I began as an only child with an only language. This language was English and Spanish.

My English and Spanish came from a pact my parents made. My father, a green-eyed American, agreed to speak to me in English. My mother, a Mexican by birth, a feminist by choice, promised to speak to me in her native Romance language peppered with Nahuatl.

Their pact gave me lots of words. Folger's crystals. Asshole. Aguacate. Tiliche. Cadillac. Smart. Girl. Sanguich. That's Mexican for *sandwich.*

I spoke my first words at a place more American than Appomattox, the McDonald's across from the Greyhound bus station. This makes me a patriot, though the words themselves were Francophile.

"French fry," I moaned, reaching for one.

French fry: those are a lot of consonant clusters for a small mouth.

French fry. Papa francesa. Pomme frite. Joan of Arc.

While Mom drew blood at the hospital and Dad worked teaching fourth graders, I amused myself at nursery school. From its playground, I saw tombstones, monuments, and an American flag waving at the cemetery. I got down on all fours and knelt in the dirt by the swings. I stared at a gopher hole, wanting to slide my fist down it. The hole proved very tempting for one boy. He sexually assaulted it and they took him away in an ambulance.

I enjoyed the cuisine at nursery school; it tasted metallic since it all came from cans, even the juice. I hated naptime.

Naptime was torture.

I wanted to move and talk during naptime, but I couldn't. I forced myself to stay still and shut my eyes. I listened to other kids breathe. I peeked at the ceiling and at light making its way through thin cracks between curtains. I wondered about the cemetery. The mats were soft and smelled like children who drank juice.

Dad forgot to pick me up once. I didn't mind. Dusk was coming and a nursery school teacher and I sat together at a short table. We stared at a wall clock.

I smiled and told her, "I wonder what happens here at night." I imagined toys, books, blankets, chairs, and cans becoming enchanted, performing for me after dark. I asked, "Do you think things come to life and move?"

The nursery school teacher laughed.

She said, "They might."

The door opened. Dad stood there. "I'm sorry!" he said. As he explained the reason for his tardiness, I zoned out, fantasizing about enchanted objects, disappointed that I would be sleeping in my own bed and not a nursery school cupboard.

Dad laughed at the way my nursery school teachers treated me.

My language paradox escaped them.

They didn't get that my first language was double theirs.

Dad discovered their misunderstanding as we set the dinner table one night. I pointed. In a didactic tone, I narrated, "This is a plate. This is a cup. This is a spoon. This is a fork." I gestured and continued, "This is a chair. This is a table. This is the kitchen."

Dad's brow furrowed. He watched and listened. I grabbed his hand, walked him around the house, and introduced him to more domestic nouns: "This is a lamp. This is a television. This is dust. This is a sofa."

Eventually, he laughed.

Mom was in the kitchen. He shouted, "Guess what!" at her.

"Qué?"

"The nursery school ladies think Myriam can't speak English so they're trying to teach her! They've turned her into a parrot!"

Dad spoke the truth. This was *exactly* what had happened.

On my first day, yo hablé con mis nursery school maestras usando palabras como éstas because I assumed we all had the same words. I didn't know I was spewing ciphers fed to me by a foreigner. I didn't know Mexicans *were* Mexicans, a category some mistake for subhuman, a category my grandfather mistakes for divine. I thought of myself as a person, and I understood people. People were people, and people talked, and talking was for everyone. Today, I understand that words are for everyjuan, but that not everyjuan is for every word, so please, dear reader, si no te molesta demasiado, pass me the metaphorical french fries as you whisper what you wish had been the first un-American words to pass through your uncorrupted lips.

The Whites

It took me years to figure out that white people are white people and that that's not necessarily a good thing.

Having white neighbors began the process. Their lifestyle differed from ours.

They looked different from us. Mom, Dad, and I were brunettes. The whites had yellow hair. They used fewer words than we did.

Mom sometimes went over to the whites' to practice her English.

She sat across from the white mom at her coffee table. In contrast to one another, each became Other. A mother from another Other.

While they visited, Mom sipped black coffee. She kissed burgundy lipstick stains onto her mug. Her hair, which she parted down the middle, reached her breast pockets. Liquid liner that tapered into tails highlighted her brown eyes. Mom's bone structure put the white mom's to shame. Her cheekbones were so *there* and lushly sculpted that they made the white mom's face look like mashed potatoes from a box. Not that the white mom was ugly. Her face just didn't exude foreign-lady sexiness the way Mom's did. The white mom's face exuded Puritanism. Margarine. Thrift. The absence of fun.

Mom met Dad in Mexico back when he had long hair and wore bell-bottoms. She first laid eyes on him as he walked past a Guadalajara cemetery, and she knew. She turned to her big sister and said, "See that hippie walking across the street? I'm going to marry him."

Her sister reminded her, "You have a boyfriend."

Mom said, "So?"

Mom broke up with her boyfriend and courted Dad with marigolds. She proposed to him and they married in a Catholic temple designed by one of Mom's uncles. Dad was working at the American School, teaching English and music to the kids of politicians and moguls, and his students filled the pews at his wedding. As a gift, one boy offered my newlywed parents a Great Dane. Dad declined, explaining that he could not feed it on a teacher's salary.

Dad applied to graduate schools in the u.s. and got accepted to one in Tucson. He quit the American School, Mom quit her job as a chemist, and they traveled to Arizona, where they made me in the dry heat.

I guess Gila monsters and saguaros are aphrodisiacs.

Dad earned a master's in linguistics, and then he and Mom left the southwest. They moved to Santa Maria, California, a super-quiet place that grew strawberries and needed teachers.

Strawberries and broccoli grew across the street from our house. A donkey lived at the end of the road.

The white people lived to our left.

Their skin nearly matched their hair.

They parked a long RV in their driveway. They ate lots of Jell-O. The white mom teased her hair into yellow swan wings. It looked great. The white dad looked like my uncle who smoked a lot of mota. Their white son was super chill and fun to hang out with. I followed him around his yard, staring up at his metallic hair, longing for him to show me affection. A smile. Meanwhile, his little sister acted cunty.

One time, when I was playing with her in our driveway, Dad told her, "That's a pretty dress you're wearing."

She looked at him with nonchalance. "I know," she said.

Her answer mortified Dad. At the dinner table that night, he kept saying, "She was supposed to say thank you. She was supposed to say thank you."

I eventually convinced the white boy, Josh, to play with me. I wanted him to myself, so when his sister, Emily, asked, "Can I play, too?" I told her, "No."

Her lower lip quivered. Tears spilled down her cheeks. They landed on her homemade dress.

"Eat your lip gloss," I told her.

I reached into her pocket and pulled out her lip gloss tin. I slid open its lid and eased my finger into the purple sludge. I helped myself to a serving, rubbed it across my thick lips, and sucked the excess off my finger.

I was three, maybe four.

Makeup meant for children is always a snack.

// //

"Live from New York . . ."

This must have been an omen: Mom went into labor with me while Dad was watching *Saturday Night Live*. He was laughing so hard at John Belushi dressed like a bee that he didn't hear the screams. Mom's Yorkie bit his ankle and barked. He frowned, got up, and followed her to the bedroom. From the doorway, Dad stared at Mom. The bed glowed red from her blood. Dad wrapped her in wet sheets and threw her into the Pinto. He sped to the hospital, where a doctor wearing a leisure suit sunk his scalpel into Mom's abdomen. He cut a slit, reached between the lips, pulled me out, and held my blue body. He spanked me. I halfheartedly breathed.

This set the tone for the rest of my life.

Mom got pregnant again before I started kindergarten. Dad broke it to me at the kitchen table. He sipped black coffee. I commented, "That smells good, Daddy."

"Take a sip," he said. He held out the cup.

I took it and sipped. I tasted masculinity.

"Mommy is going to have a baby," said Dad. "What do you want, a brother or a sister?"

"Yes," I prophesied.

Doctors had to cut out the twins, a boy and a girl, three months early because of complications. A pilot helicoptered Mom to a hospital in Palo Alto, and Dad threw my things in a suitcase while his forehead and bald spot dewed. Mine remained dry. I was fine. Mom being gone and Dad having to go with her didn't bother me. I got that it was important for Dad to go be with Mom, and I kind of got that something very bad might be happening, something that might prevent my mom from ever coming back, but I wasn't upset by it. I was excited. The abandonment felt like an adventure. My parents were leaving me. This would be new and fun. Kind of like being an orphan.

Anyone who isn't an orphan has orphan fantasies.

Dad walked me up the driveway with the RV.

He handed my suitcase and me over to the white mom.

She smiled. She said, "You'll stay with Emily."

I thought about what this meant.

This meant I was going to get to sleep in Emily's room.

Emily lived in a room meant for an object. Lace edged her bedspread and curtains. Mahogany furniture carved with rosebuds gleamed. Pink accents lurked everywhere. Her carpet was a crotchy color. The room's femininity was inescapable. From a Victorian cradle by the bed, a porcelain doll's eyes stared at the popcorn ceiling. The things in her room were teaching Emily how to be a woman.

I crawled into Emily's bed and felt deficient. I was wearing a scratchy, nosebleed-stained nightshirt. Emily was luxuriating in a gown as white as her race. It was like what Nellie Oleson wore in that episode of *Little House on the Prairie* where she pretends to be a paraplegic and sits in that beautiful wheelchair. Staring at Emily's curtains, I didn't contemplate my mother's impending death. I thought about how I could get my hands on Emily's stuff.

I was very curious about how the whites handled food. At home, we typically ate fusion. Mom cooked hamburgers, meat loaf, and pork chops, but she defiled these foods in ethnically specific ways. She sprinkled radishes and stuck avocado slices where they didn't belong.

I was loafing in the kitchen when the white mom told me, "Since you're gonna be staying with us til . . ." she paused to choose her words, "your parents get back, you're gonna help us out. Today, you're gonna help make dinner."

"What're we having?"

The white mom smiled. She said, "Since you're visiting, Mexican."

I imagined the Mexican foods Mom sometimes made. Enchiladas melting in glass dishes. Chuletas with onions floating in red sauce. Chicken tacos fried in corn oil. Pozole. Machaca. Mom never made mole. In English, that's an animal. It can't see.

"What are we having?" I repeated.

"Mexican casserole."

Casserole was a new word for me. It intrigued me. It sounded musical.

The white mom putzed around the kitchen dicing, blanching, and massaging things into a glass dish that she carried to the oven and slid onto a rack. I shut the door on it and watched the casserole warm through a greasy porthole.

The white mom grabbed five goblets from a cupboard and set them on the counter. I helped her layer cream and red Jell-O, which Mom pronounced *yellow,* into them. We made seductive parfaits the likes of which I'd never seen in our kitchen. Our kitchen was a chocolate pudding place.

I couldn't wait to explore these cool desserts with a cold spoon.

Dinnertime came and we sat around the table in the dining room, which was basically an extension of the kitchen but a step up. The house had a split-level floor plan. The white mom stabbed the casserole with her spatula. Her vigor made her swan wings flap. She scooped a square onto each of our plates and ladled the night's vegetable, soggy brussels sprouts, out of another glass dish. Four green balls rolled beside my casserole hunk.

My fork stabbed my casserole and brought it to my mouth. I dropped it on my tongue. There was nothing Mexican about it. Its spices told unfamiliar stories, but I used my milk as a chaser and managed to choke it down without vomiting. The brussels sprouts were a different story. I scooped one into my mouth and realized its flavor: eternal damnation. I parted my lips and dropped my jaw. The vegetable rolled off my tongue. It fell back onto the plate. It glistened with my spit.

"I can't eat these," I told the white mom.

"Why not?"

"I don't want to talk about it. I just can't eat them."

"If you don't eat them, you can't have dessert."

I could not believe her nerve. She was blackmailing me and I had done her a gigantic favor by eating her casserole, whose nationality was a lie.

"I can't do it," I reiterated.

The white mom rose and strutted across the dining room to the kitchen. She pulled open the fridge door, took out the tray of parfaits, and carried them over. She placed one in front of her husband, one in front of Emily, and one in front of Josh. She segregated the one that would be mine on the counter. She set a long-handled spoon beside it. Its metal clinking against tile practically neiner neinered.

"Once you finish your brussels sprouts," she said, "you can have dessert."

"But I helped make dinner! I helped make those!"

"You have to eat your vegetables."

I watched the others wolf their parfaits down and lick their spoons. I watched the white mom clear the dishes. I watched the back of her yellow head as she washed and dried. I looked down at her brussels sprouts. They looked cold and evil. They looked like American presidents. I trusted my instincts. I refused them entry into my face. They remained on my plate, unloved.

The white mom looked at the clock hanging on the wall by the sliding glass door. The big hand rested on eleven. The little hand rested on twelve.

"Go put on your pajamas," she finally conceded.

My win made me feel glad, but what had my victory cost me?

Mom saying *yellow,* a goblet of Jell-O.

Judas and Icarus

My first touch came from a white man's spanking.

My first crush was my white neighbor Josh.

My first friend, my best friend, was white, too.

We met in kindergarten, and I loved her when I was five, I loved her when I was six, I loved her when I was seven, I loved her when I was eight, I loved her when I was nine, I loved her when I was ten, I loved her when I was eleven, I loved her when I was twelve, and I loved her when I was thirteen. I have loved her up till now, and I have loved her in the future.

She once smoked crack on accident. She thought it was heroin.

// //

Sometimes, I imagine Krakow filled with quaint Polish crack houses.

// //

The white girl who smoked crack on accident is named Ida.

We met in kindergarten at Montessori school. I didn't like her immediately. She was too much like me. A cunt. A free thinker. A roamer.

Montessori school is great if you're a liberated person. It's a great place to be if you're obstinate and don't appreciate being told what to say, think, feel, or do. Montessori school is private and everything in it is child size. I hung out in this miniature world for two years, and every school day I got to choose what I wanted to do with myself. If I wanted to sit in a beanbag paging through a thesaurus for hours, I could. If I wanted to show picture books to our school pet, a bored corn snake named Ivan, I could. I could hunch over long division problems, breaking down numbers till it was time for recess or lunch. At lunch, I lolled beneath our playground ginkgo tree, collecting leaves and unsurreptitiously smelling my fingers.

Montessori school ruined me for normal school and life in general. It made me only want to do things I care about or am curious about. Which is really hard if you have to live in reality.

Ida and I migrated to public school for second grade. Our parents didn't like how our Montessori school got increasingly traditional as the grades got higher, so they figured they'd just stick us in normal school anyway.

We were assigned to the same class, and it was there that our love really began to flourish. We recognized our own selves in the other. We recognized ourselves as refugees. We were both new to the land of raising your hand to go to the bathroom.

This was a trickier culture.

But still cool.

Second grade mirrored Montessori. We couldn't roam the school, but we could roam the room. I could talk and ramble as a much as I had to. Nobody told me to shut up or wrote my name on the board for being bad. My teacher, peers, and classroom pets tolerated my garrulousness. I sat beside Ida.

We read books together.

Third grade came and changed everything.

Our teacher, Mrs. De Leon, expected us to stay in our desks. We had to raise our hands for permission to stroll to the pencil sharpener, a fine place to fart. An amateurish painting of the night sky hung by our classroom door. I often stared at it and thought, "I've seen better." I later saw that painting of the night sky in a collection of works by van Gogh.

Thanks to Montessori, and genetics, I didn't know how to be quiet. I felt compelled in a way that itched and burned to turn everything in my head into spoken word. I had to give my words to somebody, and I did, I gave them to everyone, and Mrs. De Leon did not approve. I talked without raising my hand, and she wrote my name on the board. She put check marks next to it as I talked more. She moved me from desk to desk to desk. She sat me beside introverts and recent arrivals from Sinaloa. Her changes of venue did nothing to quiet me. The shy became my audience. I got through to the Mexicans. I told them tall tales and discussed American current events with them . . . in Spanish.

Ida and I spent recesses in the baseball dugout. This was in the southeast corner of the grassy field we jogged or walked laps around for PE. Bees buzzed in it. Frogs died in it. A chain-link fence ringed the field and the backyards of tract homes pressed against one edge while a manmade pine forest grew along another. Pine needles formed a carpet that made crispy noises as our Velcro shoes crept.

Ida and I sat on the dugout's wooden bench, imagining. Three other girls, Emiko, Madi, and Espie, joined us in our mental adventures. We spent so much time in that dugout making a sport of imagining that our minds melded. We formed a community. One day, I said, "This is a club."

It felt good to be in a club. During club, we told stories, harvested clover, killed bees, invented fantasylands inspired by Dungeons and Dragons, and developed rituals. We sacrificed snails and stuck their meat on Ritz crackers. Ida dared me, "Eat it."

I popped escargot in my mouth. I chewed and swallowed.

The five of us were having so much fun partying in the dugout that it attracted the stupider sex. Some wandered into our meeting spot.

A boy interrupted me. It asked, "Can we be in your club?"

"No," I answered. "It's girls only."

"That's not fair," Steve, the boy, protested. He was Mexican and had what are commonly called piercing blue eyes. It happens.

"He's right," agreed Emiko. "It's not fair."

"OK," I said. I looked from Emiko to Steve. I stared into his blue eyes with fortitude. "You and your friends can join our club if you climb to the top of this." I pointed to the chain-link backstop that reached several stories high. "And jump."

The rational boys in Steve's group sighed. Those with high levels of T sprinted for the backstop. Their fingers curled around its metal and their tennis shoes slipped in and out of its holes. They moved farther and farther up, and the blowing of whistles made us look across the field, at the playground. The yard-duty ladies gestured with their arms. The huge-titted one jogged toward us. Her breasts dog-paddled in her muumuu. She slowed near second base.

"Stop!" she screamed at the climbers. "Get DOWN!"

One climber, Reymundo, in English, KING OF THE WORLD, what hubris in a name, froze. He dangled. He swiveled his head and looked over his right shoulder, at me. He looked at the yard-duty lady. He blinked. One foot moved after the other as he felt his way back to earth.

Steve clung halfway up the backstop. He stared down at us. He looked at the yard-duty lady. He looked back at the sky. He scrambled up.

I hoped Steve would injure himself and die so that I wouldn't have to let him into my club. That had been my strategy. To give his sex an insurmountable initiation. Like the literacy tests given to black folks in the American South before the Voting Rights Act passed.

I was an early-onset feminist.

Steve reached the backstop's sharply angled crown. He paused.

"Don't you dare!" threatened the yard-duty lady. To a third-grade boy, those words equal *please.*

Steve's fingers uncoiled. His white T-shirt flew up. It flapped as he fell. I spied his belly button. Unlike most people's, his pushed forward into a repugnant outie.

Steve's feet touched down near home plate. Dirt hardly puffed into the air around his jeans. I'd expected him to shatter or liquefy, but he was feline. He landed fine.

"Fuck," I thought to myself. "He's in."

The yard-duty lady herded us across the baseball diamond, grass, clover, playground sand, blacktop, and cement. We filed into our classroom and sat at our desks. I felt warm in my sweat pants. Our teacher paced the bald carpet. Her gaze zeroed in on Steve. She demanded, "Why did you do that?"

Steve pointed his finger at me. "She told me to," he said. "So that I could join her club."

Mrs. De Leon's gaze fixed upon me. "Is that true?" she asked.

I nodded.

She returned her stern expression to Steve. She asked, "If she told you to jump from a cliff, would you do it?"

"No," he said.

"Good. You're suspended."

I grinned. Mrs. De Leon looked at me, shook her head, and said, "No more club."

I felt slightly crushed but satisfied. I'd rather have my club destroyed by a strict third-grade teacher than let fucking boys into it.

The Problem of Evil

It's OK to be mean.

Dad taught me so, as he stood at the kitchen counter, playing with his watch. I poured a glass of milk, gargled, and gulped. I'd emerged from my bedroom after paging through *A Child's Book of Saints*. Reading about morality had made me thirsty. I swished milk between my cheeks, warming it, and thought about the book's martyrs and mystics. I admired them, especially the girls, but a pattern troubled me. Bad things happened to the saintliest ones. Villagers lit them on fire. Pirates and aristocrats raped them. Barbarians carved their breasts and noses off. It seemed that the nicer you were, especially during the Middle Ages, the meaner the world was.

"Dad?" I said.

"Yes?"

"Why does evil exist?"

"Just a second," he answered.

He multitasked, pondering my inquiry while fiddling with his watch. The lack of a quick response made me uneasy.

Through my milk moustache, I blurted, "Why does god let so many bad things happen?"

I breathed through my mouth. Waited.

Dad looked at me with the same face he made when I questioned the Easter Bunny's existence. In a matter-of-fact voice, he said, "Myriam, think of how boring life would be if nothing bad ever happened."

His words felt epiphanic. I smiled and my heart felt very, very warm. It was bathing in permission.

What an excellent point. Why hadn't I arrived at that conclusion?

Dad's words rehabilitated bad things. His logic made them beautiful. Necessary, in fact.

It isn't just greed that's good. Mean is good too. Being mean makes us feel alive. It's fun and exciting. Sometimes, it keeps us alive.

// //

W. H. Auden wrote that evil is unspectacular. I totally disagree. Evil is dazzling. If it's done right, mean can be dazzling too.

// //

We act mean to defend ourselves from boredom and from those who would chop off our breasts. We act mean to defend our clubs and institutions. We act mean because we like to laugh. Being mean to boys is fun and a second-wave feminist duty. Being rude to men who deserve it is a holy mission. Sisterhood is powerful, but being a bitch is more exhilarating. Being a bitch is spectacular.

// //

Being mean isn't for everybody.

It's best practiced by those who understand it as an art form.

These virtuosos live closer to the divine. They're queers.

To observe the queer art of being mean, watch *Paris Is Burning*.

Venus Xtravaganza, a trans woman who's murdered partway through the documentary, inspires me to be a better mean. In a scene where she's so beautifully lit she looks like a painting, Venus cries, "You wanna talk about reading? Let's talk about reading!" She embodies her femininity with cruel genius and shakes her peroxided mane. She rubs her fingers down her creamy arms. Her skin's beauty reminds me of good, soft things—peaches, magic hour sunlight, babies that never cry. She yells, "Touch this skin, darling, touch this skin, honey! Touch all of this skin! OK? You just can't take it! You're just an overgrown orangutan." She pronounces *orangutan* so that each syllable awakens and develops a soul.

Drag queen Dorian Corey also demonstrates the high art of meanness during her interviews. New York learned the extent of it after AIDS killed her. Friends were cleaning out her home and found a mummified hustler among her sequins and feathers. Somebody had wrapped his corpse in imitation leather and stuffed it in a trunk. Shrouding him in pleather was perhaps the cruelest part of the violence.

When was the last time you were mean for fun? When was the last time you were mean in the name of politics? Have you ever been mean for Jesus? When was the last time you tried to kill someone rather than let him into your club? When was the last time you wanted to kill someone but chose to be a bitch instead of a murderer?

Have you been called a bitch?

Dad has gotten so pissed at Mom, my sister, and me that he has called us bitches.

When he calls us this word, I want to say, "Dad, we're just making your life more interesting. Remember?"

Googolplex

Although Ida was white, she sort of wasn't.

She looked like Kurt Cobain. She attended bilingual classes with me and spoke and understood Spanish. She kicked it with Mexicans on the playground and learned how to play handball. When she came over to my house, she slurped Mom's pozole instead of asking "What is this?" in that supremely bitchy California-girl accent some white girls reserved for interrogating my mother's hospitality.

The fifth-grade race war proved Ida's racial solidarity.

An Asian American child fired the first shots.

She stood near me in the playground sand by the handball courts. She looked me up and down and said, "Your mother . . . is a wetback."

I lost control of my limbs. My hands attacked her and they shoved her chest, making her lose her balance and fall to the sand. My toes flew into her stomach. My Velcro shoes landed blow after blow, her round face winced, and the bell rang. Recess was over. I quit kicking. She ran away crying.

She didn't tell any grown-ups what had happened, but the fifth-grade girls balkanized soon after. White girls from the English-only classes refused to socialize with girls from the bilingual classes. Looking at the jungle gym and tetherball courts, our segregation was clear as melanin. Clusters of girls named Lupe played together. Clusters of girls named Michelle played together. Lupes and Michelles didn't mix. The playground felt dicey and tribal.

From the jungle-gym bars, a dangling white girl, Amy, called, "Go back to Baja!"

Her taunt seemed aimed at both Ida and me.

We paused beside the merry-go-round. I turned to Ida. "Have you ever been to Mexico?" I asked her.

Ida shook her head. "No," she answered. "But I'd go with you."

"You would love it," I told her. "The food is really good there. My uncle got his head cut off by a bus. The cockroaches fly."

"Really?"

I nodded.

Amy screamed, "Ida loves wetbacks!"

Ida screamed back, "Fuck your mother in the tit!"

I felt like hugging Ida. I'm not sure where she learned that comeback. Her mother did work for a gynecologist. Her father lived in Colorado and worked for the defense industry. Ida was so smart. Her favorite number was googolplex.

The balkanization and screaming drew our teachers outside. They decided they needed to fix things. They informed us that we were going to have to sit down and "talk about it."

After lunch, a male teacher marched the boys to the blacktop to play dodgeball. Girls got herded into the English-only classroom. I stared at the boys through tinted windows. My skin felt jealous. I didn't want to be inside.

"So," prodded the English-only teacher. "What's going on?"

She stood by the board. She folded her arms.

She was dressed entirely in purple.

The white girls sat on the opposite side of the classroom, in desks facing ours. They blinked at us. We blinked back.

I raised my hand. The English-only teacher said, "Go ahead."

I pointed at the lot of them and said, "They call us wetbacks and tell us to go back to Mexico. Those girls are racists. And she's not even Mexican." I pointed at Ida.

Ida nodded.

White lower lips quivered. White eyes grew glassy. One by one, white girls burst into tears. Ida and all the Mexican girls looked at each other, like, seriously?

"Apologize for making them cry," said the English-only teacher.

"Sorry," I said without any sincerity.

Señorita

Soon after the fifth-grade race war ended, we unloaded boxes from a moving truck and hauled them into our new address.

Some of our boxes held Mexican knickknacks and some of our boxes held Polish knickknacks and our family became the first thusly inter-racial family to pioneer this upper-middle-class neighborhood in the name of those like ourselves, Mexican Polacks. We became the first in our neighborhood to blanket long, hot kielbasas in tortillas. In the kitchen, accidentally cutting her finger while dicing an onion, Mom tainted the bulb with her blood. Dad stood at the stove and stirred a cauldron of pork broth. He dropped a garlic clove into the simmering and interrupted the lecture he was giving me on semiotics.

"Hey!" he shouted at Mom. "Hey!" he repeated. He looked at her bloody onion. "Don't get AIDS in my dinner!"

He was joking, of course. Mom didn't have AIDS. My gay cousin did.

// //

Can you smell yourself? I can usually smell myself, but sometimes I can't. I have heard some people say that different races have different smells. If you're interracial, do you have a blended fragrance? My crotch has a blended fragrance. I love the way it smells, especially when it hasn't been washed in a few days. It smells like life, the ocean, baked goods, and shawarma.

This white lesbian from Kalamazoo once told me that when she was taking an ethnic studies class in high school, the teacher told the kids of color that they could say anything they wanted about white people for one class period and not get in trouble. The white lesbian told me that a COC, a classmate of color, demanded, "Why do white people smell like wet dogs?"

I don't think white people smell like wet dog. But white people's houses do have a smell. The smell is sour and not very alive. Like a phonebook.

I walked home with white kids from our new neighborhood's bus stop. They failed to pick up on my smell (kielbasa and corn tortillas), and one of these kids, a white girl, turned shameless in her curiosity. I'm going to call this white girl Shaquanda. White people love to appropriate things. By naming the white girl Shaquanda I'm beating them at their own game.

Shaquanda stared hard at my profile. She scrutinized my nose, cheeks, lips, and eyelashes. In her deeply bitchy California-girl accent, she terrorized me.

She asked, "What are you?"

To keep it simple, I answered, "Mexican."

Shaquanda scowled. This made her look smarter than she was. It also made her look like her mother, a big-boned pro-life activist brave enough to picket Planned Parenthood while wearing cow print.

"Are you sure you're not Filipina?" asked Shaquanda. "We had a Filipina who cleaned our house and she looked like you."

I said, "It's safe to say I'm not Filipina," and wondered about my safety.

Shaquanda listened to me breathe. She was checking to see if I breathed in English or some other language. Breaths do happen in different languages. They are onomatopoetry. Even animal onomatopoetics happen in different languages. American dogs say "woof." Mexican dogs say "guau." Spanglish dogs say "go Raiders."

Shaquanda and I went to junior high together. Almost everyone there was a stranger. Almost everyone there was white. The elementary school where I'd come from had been about fifty-fifty, about half Mexican, half white, and a few of everybody else.

Ida wasn't among these new whites. She went to the mostly Mexican junior high by the freeway. She was going to have the joy of entering puberty among cholas.

The pallor of my junior high's student body worked as my weight-loss pill. Digesting the sight of so many white kids made my hands tremble. I sweated. My heart raced. At night, in bed, I stared at the black hole of my ceiling, knowing that in the daylight, I'd see nothing as infinite, familiar, and dark as it.

In the morning, back on campus, I locked myself in bathroom stalls and diarrheaed my baby fat away. I flushed but did not emerge reborn as a swan. I was thinner but still tan. I wanted to kill that color. Undoing it would take dedication. It would take turning goth to undo. It would take sitting in the shade while reading vampire erotica to undo. It would take wearing veiled hats and tubes of skin lightening creams bought from Mexican pharmacies. It would take me years to be able to declare victory over my complexion.

My classmates took my brownness as a warning. It told them that I was a thief. At lunchtime, they hugged their brown bags to their chests when I walked past.

A skater standing near the cafeteria doors grinned at me. His freckles tricked me into thinking he was sweet.

"Nigger lips," he hissed at my face.

Isn't it something how an "oversized" body part, even if it's not black, "darkens" you? I inherited my Niger lips from my half-Polish father. My eyes came from him, too—green. He gave me chlorophyll. Our eyes photosynthesize. They catch energy. They release it.

The school counselor enrolled me in PE, pre-algebra, life science, English, art, and history, and in history, I recognized the boy suffering near the globe. With prowess adding bounce to my step, I walked to him. I prayed we might knit an alliance. This boy was already intimate with my lips. He knew they were soft and mean.

Macaulay grinned and panted. His breath warmed sub-Saharan Africa.

Macaulay and I knew each other from a simpler time and place, second grade. We'd scissored and glued together in class, and during recesses we'd competed against one another in timed tournaments of sexual assault. Our playground sport was called Kissy Boys versus Kissy Girls. Its object was to chase down an "oppositely sexed" team member and connect lips with any part of them. A kiss benched the receiving player till only the toughest kiss rapist was left standing. Due to my well-developed calves, ambition, and machismo, my ass rarely warmed the bench.

One afternoon, after a sweaty session of Kissy Boys versus Kissy Girls, we lined up outside our classroom. Spent, we panted, a chorus of perverts. How moist we must have been. Our class pets, a nuclear guinea pig family, were going to replace their salt licks with our faces.

I heard my name and turned. Macaulay's face careened at mine. His mouth banged into my lips, and my teeth dug into my own wet flesh. This was an unsanctioned kiss, we were off the kissy clock, and this was the only time Macaulay kissed me in this way. He disappeared from my life after second grade and reappeared in history. He became a part of history, mine and Mr. Hand's.

Mr. Hand, our seventh-grade history teacher, stood in front of the blackboard. Before him, rows of empty tables stretched to the back wall. We stood against this wall on the first day. We waited.

"You've got about thirty seconds to choose a seat!" he cried. "Hustle!"

I figured Mr. Hand was exaggerating, but I grabbed Macaulay's elbow and tugged him up an aisle to the left front corner. I slid onto a hard yellow chair. Macaulay slid onto the chair to my left. To our left, sunlight streamed through a wall that was almost all window. Our profiles warmed.

Since he was blue-eyed, and likely had a penis, everyone had taken Mr. Hand seriously. Everyone had claimed a seat and was waiting in silence. Give-us-more-instructions was our vibe. Tell us what to do. Mr. Hand lumbered, knock-kneed, along the front row. He tossed syllabi. I scooped them off my tabletop, kept two, and passed the rest to the girl behind me.

I turned back to face the front but peeked at my neighbor.

Macaulay's auburn hair, ermine eyes, and almost olive skin were the same, but something, perhaps a trauma, had turned him into a mouth breather. With each breath, his lips got drier and grosser. Braces gave him a snout that would've looked cute on a marsupial. On him, it looked both awkward and slightly sinister.

Macaulay's sweater drew my gaze. Its sheepskin collar fluffed around his neck so that his head seemed spit out of a mushroom cloud crafted from innocence. The sheepskin was so thick, full, and fluffy that I felt lewd impulses toward it. I wanted to touch the fleece. I wanted to squeeze it the way I sometimes longed to squeeze big boobs. Have you ever wanted to milk a well-endowed lady? Seriously milk her?

I sat on my hands and swung my feet. They failed to reach the carpet.

Under the table, a sensation intruded.

It was happening near my bicycle shorts' hem. Every girl and her mother was wearing bicycle shorts then so everyone could, therefore, appraise the cloven heft of generation upon generation of camel toe. Camel toes were pleased that a fad had brought them into the light. Camel toes basked in the ultraviolet rays of 1989.

I looked at Macaulay with caution. This trepidation was new but it felt natural. Instinctual. I knew that what was happening under the table shouldn't have been happening, but my impulses did not command me to fight. I froze. Many animals do this. Deer. Possum. My mother.

With nonchalance, Macaulay stared ahead, at the bulletin board.

Against its yellow butcher paper, the word *welcome* hung in chunky black. Pins jammed into each cutout letter, suspending the collection. Mr. Hand must've tracked, hunted, and captured his *w*, the two *e*'s, and *l, c, o,* and *m*. Or maybe he caught two *w*'s and flipped one upside down.

My brother, Herman, owned a similar collection. He hunted flies, moths, and dragonflies with nets. He scavenged dead insects off windowsills. He skewered his bug collection with needles. Another way of looking at the pins jamming into *welcome* was that Mr. Hand believed in acupuncture for language.

I noticed movement.

The hand Macaulay wasn't molesting me with rose to his snout.

Four of its fingers curled into a circle with the index finger pointing at the ceiling. This pointer pressed flat against his mouth. From this dry hole issued the most brazen yet muted "Shh."

The hand that was molesting me slid to my inner thigh and squeezed the fat. Sensing that if I yelped, I'd look like the bad guy, I obeyed the shh. I swallowed my chance at rescue.

// //

The reason I know that Mr. Hand taught history was "History" was the name of his class.

I didn't learn much history from him. My time with him mostly taught me how to be quietly molested. The word *molester* makes me think of animals. Molesters are bad moles that touch other moles. A molester creeps up the tunnel behind unsuspecting mammals and lets his whiskers slip where they don't belong.

When his prey asks, "What are you doing?" the molester answers, "Oh, I didn't see you there."

Which is true.

Because of his snout, Macaulay looked like a mole, and he'd scoot his chair so his was touching mine. Our tabletop masked his incursions, and I'd bite down on nothing, pressing my molars together till I felt the hand that he'd plopped on my knee slide toward and into my pudding.

Once Macaulay began stirring, my tapioca warmed and bubbled. I didn't want it to be warm. I didn't want it to be cooking in public, and class is public, very public, and I had a feeling that if one of my classmates noticed what was happening to me under the table, they'd call me a ho.

// //

I was having my usual diarrhea and reading accusations carved into the bathroom stall paint.

Many accusations involved the word *hoe* and sometimes a girl was a hoe and at other times she was a ho. Spellings varied. According to the stall door, some teachers were even hoes and hos. And according to an accusation carved into the small metal coffin that received our blood-drenched sanitary napkins, our woodshop teacher fingerbanged himself.

// //

Dad and I gardened together on the weekends.

Recently, I'd helped him plant five sugar bushes along our front yard hillside. Bush wasn't the only thing Dad and I handled together. Dad also taught me how to handle leaves, dirt, and grass. He Three-Stoogeishly taught me to mow. Maternally, he taught me to hoe. Mexicanly, he taught me to blow—leaf blow. Maybe mowing, hoeing, and blowing were why I was feeling certain mole feelings lately. Like a molester, I wanted to bump into girls so that I could press myself against their soft parts. The chipmunks napping between their thighs. I knew girls had chipmunks between their legs because I was a girl and I had a chipmunk there, too. These creatures seek out nuts. They hoard fetuses for the winter.

Macaulay licked his snout. He leaned into my earlobe.

"Have you got a big, hairy bush?" he asked.

"What?"

In a blue-balls tone, he insisted, "A big, hairy bush! Do you have a big, sweet bush?"

"We have five," I whispered.

Macaulay's breath picked up like he'd hit a jackpot. His hand groped for the bushes I'd been hiding from him.

// //

Mr. Hand wheeled the TV/VCR cart in front of the board. Its presence announced FUCK TEACHING!

Mr. Hand's knuckles pushed down the VCR's lid and pressed buttons. A taped episode of *The Simpsons* came on.

This was a form of Christmas, watching cartoons instead of having class, and for my pussy, there was an extra dose of merriment. The gift Mr. Hand was giving us was so great that Macaulay felt no need to fondle mine.

I consider every pussy a gift.

I glanced at Macaulay's hands.

They were out in public instead of down in pubic. They rested on our tabletop.

Thank you, Homer, Bart, Lisa, and Marge.

// //

News about somewhere oily barked in the background. Kuwait.

Dad was scooping a food I associated with euthanasia onto his plate. He looked up from his lima beans. He asked me, "How was school?"

Before I could weigh the implications of my blurt, I Touretted, "We watched *The Simpsons,* and tomorrow, we're watching more!"

Dad's beard bristled. It asked, "You watched cartoons at school? Which class?"

// //

No TV/VCR cart. Just Mr. Hand with skin glowing like grilled salmon. The glow plus the way he was grasping his chalk, with a lot of ill will, worried me.

The bell rolled its long, high-pitched *rr*. Mr. Hand made a point of surveying our faces, acknowledging the disappointment. He said, "We were going to watch more *Simpsons,* but we can't." The groan of children who've been let down, and have, thus, lost a certain innocence, motivated Mr. Hand to behave childishly. He looked at me. His blue-eyed stare ratted me out.

"Somebody's parents called to complain," he said.

I felt like an asshole, but I didn't feel like my parents were assholes. I knew they were right—you don't go to school to watch cartoons, even if these cartoons keep you from getting molested. Mr. Hand maintained eye contact with me long enough to damn me.

// //

As punishment, Mr. Hand was going to make us learn.

He assigned us a history report and told us, "It's worth a thousand points." He walked us to the school library and dropped us off with the librarian.

Her arthritic finger pointed at the card catalogue. She said, "That's the card catalogue. It's got what you need."

This lesson on how to use the card catalogue—that it was there, along with the suggestion that we open it and take what we wanted from it—was similar to my first lesson on sex. One afternoon, Mom walked me to my room, pointed at a purple book on my bed, and said, in Spanish, "Read it."

The book was in English and I did not care for its picture of a penis.

Since the librarian was done with us, it was time to do nothing unless you were a nerd. Girls with friends went to go chew gum and talk shit. Boys with friends went to go see if they could use glasses, sunlight, and library books to start fires. Starting a fire with glasses was something I would've liked to do with friends but I didn't have any. I skulked to a table near the door and plopped into a chair that hurt every part of me.

Why does public school furniture have to hurt?

Why can it never feel good?

I opened my primary source and sighed. I looked down at it and then looked at the door. I rued having taken Mom's suggestion. When I'd asked her, "Who should I do my history report on?" she'd answered, in Spanish, "Ana Frank. Read the diary of Ana Frank."

I followed her suggestion, believing that reading a teenage girl's diary would be juicy and seductive, but it was a little slow. Anne Frank slept in an attic. She was thankful to eat dinner, though it wasn't very good. Going to the bathroom was awkward. How was this any different from going to my grandmother's house? There was even a Nazi there. Dad's mom's second husband was German. Grandma liked to play in the snow.

Boring details shoved my eyes off the page and back onto the table where an ant was marching toward a family who'd never see him again. My fingertip squished him, and I lifted him to my face. I visualized his soul leaving his many-legged body.

Someone said, "Anne Frank was a dyke."

I looked away from the bug and at the source of this interesting accusation. Gavin, a rosaceaed Little Leaguer, stood near me, grinning.

I didn't understand.

Gavin stared at me, processing. Then, he said, "You retarded Mexifart. Anne Frank was a lez."

Lez I understood. I responded to the best of my ability. I said, "Oh."

Gavin said, "Yeah, she gets it on with her friend. Anne Frank was a big-time lesbo." He physically punctuated his assertion with a hip thrust inches from my face.

"We'll see," I said.

"Lesbo . . ." Gavin whispered. To get rid of him, I pretended to read. Boys hate that shit.

// //

In Spanish, intimate apparel is called ropa interior. This directly translates to interior clothes and reminds me of the Wallace Stevens poem "Final Soliloquy of the Interior Paramour."

Wearing only ropa interior, I was reading *El Diario de Ana Frank* by lamplight. The sound of my sister snoring in the room in front of me and the sound of my brother grinding his teeth in the room to my left reminded me to think before I masturbated.

Anne Frank was talking kind of dirty. She was sharing what her body was like, but her narrative got interrupted by a photo insert featuring Jews, train stations, and Miep Gies. I pinched these pages, flipped, and got back to the meat. I dove back into Anne describing her period and confiding the texture of it, the marinaraishness of it, the minestroneishness of it. She nicknamed it her sweet secret.

Sweet secret my ass.

Anne wrote about being in bed at night and wanting to explore her body. Her hands wanted to feel up her own titties and tweak her nipples. I finally felt connected to this dead Jewish girl. I did the same thing. I played my titties. I did air guitar on them. Anne wanted to do this, but circumstances forced her to play hers acoustically.

Anne described a friend of hers. She said she got curious about this girl's body; she wanted to touch on her boobs but her friend told her no. Anne admitted to entering ecstasy when she saw figures of naked ladies, and I thought of topless Victory flying over the battlefield, a triumphant goddess nobody could squeeze.

Anne made some gay lament like, "If only I had a girlfriend! Yours, Anne."

I lowered my hand to my thingy. My finger took its temperature.

It felt like it had just come out of an oven.

// //

Macaulay's eyes were as bad as his hands. They were rubbing all over my paper, stealing what I wrote. His pencil was scratching my answers onto his paper.

Around us, a concert of pencils scratched. Pages turned to no particular rhythm.

Macaulay set his pencil down. I knew where his cheating hand was headed. I felt it land. I blushed as his fingers snuck into my crotch.

I clenched my developing jaw.

I looked at Mr. Hand.

His eyes left the page he was grading. He saw. From where he was sitting, his desk parallel to the chalkboard, his face facing us, he had a view.

Mr. Hand's eyes were watching the performance between my legs. It was symphonic. Macaulay played for no audience, but he had an audience of one.

I looked into Mr. Hand's unprepared eyes. He looked me in mine. Mr. Hand's face, neck, and scalp went from light pinkish to cherry tomato.

I'm not sure what my expression told Mr. Hand, but I think it communicated something like, "I know that seeing a boy do this to me is embarrassing for both of us, but I'm pretty sure you can make it stop."

Unable to look into a girl's eyes or soul while she was being molested, something all teachers should be prepared to confront, Mr. Hand snapped his eyes back at the worksheet he'd been grading. He hunched closer to it. He buried his blushing face in it. He used the worksheet as a veil. He became as modest as some harem girls are expected to be. As speechless, too.

Cuban Interlude

That's the story of my avant-garde molestation. I call it that because the standard American molestation narrative implicates a grown-up and not a peer, especially not a peer molesting you in broad daylight while your history teacher looks on and pretends he doesn't see. I later discovered that Macaulay did what he did to me to every girl he sat beside in junior high. Sometimes he used his foot, sometimes he used his hand, and once, he used his pencil. He was resourceful.

The way Macaulay's touch left invisible imprints on my thighs is reminiscent of Cuban artist Ana Mendieta's work. She wandered Iowa, Oaxaca, and other states, nestling her naked body into meadows, beaches, and hillsides. She created depressions then sprinkled them with things like rocks, berries, and flames. Photographs of these silhouettes remain as evidence of her interaction with the earth. You can't see her in them, but you can. You can't see Macaulay on me, but you can read him. He treated me like an artist working with dirt.

If Duchamp could place a urinal in an art gallery and thus elevate it, I can do the same thing with myself. By redefining my little molester as a sculptor, I redeem my molestation. I secrete English, Spanish, and tears, but, like a urinal, I also function as a vessel. I hold sadness, language, memories, and glee.

The other day, as I was cleaning my bedroom, I decided, for fun, to act out Mendieta's murder. Her husband, minimalist sculptor Carl Andre, pushed her out of their window. She fell, and, presumably, her body left an imprint on the roof of the delicatessen where she landed. I took off my clothes, set up my camera, and struggled against an imaginary husband. A single lamp lit my room and cast silhouettes against the wall. I held out my arms. I leaned back.

My shadow froze mid-plummet.

My camera clicked.

Art is one way to work out touch gone wrong.

// //

Somewhere on this planet, a man is touching a woman to death. Somewhere on this planet, a man is about to touch a woman to death. Men touched Mendieta and Sophia to death. In my cold bedroom, their ghosts fused. Their shadow climbed my closet door. It touched the ceiling. I felt accompanied.

There are times when I sit in my car by myself. I gaze at the passenger seat and its emptiness.

Moon glows above me. My skin prickles. Goose bumps remind me. In this emptiness, I am never alone.

Shadows fall.

Shadows fall again.

No one can touch them.

Acorn

The neighborhood we pioneered as Molacks, Mexican Polacks, remained tranquil and gorgeous. Birds purred at dawn. Eucalyptus leaves, whole carpets of them, murmured mentholated nothings. Grinning dog owners walked border collies toward sunsets made for lovers.

To the east, in fading pastels, little mountains swelled. To the west, a valley cradled our small town—named after one of Columbus's ships—a smear of beach, and the Pacific Ocean.

I'd kneel on my carpet at my tall bedroom window. I didn't look east or west. I looked ahead. I watched the grass it was my job to tend. It ended where the real plants lived, along our front yard hillside.

Across the street, to the left side of our hill, an ophthalmologist and his family lived in a fake villa. A one-eyed widow lived to the right side of our hill. She wore an eye patch and imperiled her remaining eye by hopping around her backyard tennis court with a racket. The payout from her husband's life insurance policy had bought her the court. I think her eye paid for it, too.

Vineyards grew behind these two backyards. Rows of vegetables followed the grapes. After the veggies, soft mountains—melting ice cream or mashed potatoes with butter. They created our valley.

Being surrounded by so much leisure, tranquility, and nature amplified my quiet anger. Every cell that was me was mad and jealous. The cells that were me envied the mellow that was my view, this California. I hated that the grapes glistened and dangled without anyone yanking their tendrils. The gently smiling mourning doves that sailed over our lawn pissed me off, and the sugar bushes along our driveway made me want to be them. Nobody was shoving their fingers into them. Occasionally quail families darted into them, but they came and went with such speed and lightness that the bushes only felt the suggestion of quail.

The front yard entity I had most in common with was the acorn. It kept its mouth shut. It was small. It was two toned. It held a bitterness that, in certain cases, such as ingestion by horses, poisoned, and I'd found a way to advertise my bitterness. I rolled my skirts up to the cusp of where it counted so people who were into that kind of thing could see my vertically scowling cunt. Underwear covered the cunt, but it scowled so deeply you could see it through its cotton mask.

My skirt-wearing style attracted admirers, and since Democrats were raising me, I was nice to them. (Niceness is social justice.) I led my admirers to the dirt behind the science classrooms and kissed them. One make-out partner was a man who ended up mired in the quicksand of eighth grade. He smoked cigarettes, had a rattail, rode a BMX, and wouldn't be following me to high school.

I tongue wrestled a neo-Nazi. I suspected this skinhead wanted to taste what he hated so no one could accuse him of not at least trying it. Unlocking his lips—which were surprisingly full for a racist—from mine, he leaned around my neck, toward my ear.

"You taste like chicken," he whispered.

"That's because I'm scared," I whispered back.

By eighth grade, being called a ho was water off my wet back. I was a paradoxical ho, though, a bookworm ho with a fading Mexican complexion. Young people of color are supposed to enjoy looting and eating trans fats, not sustained silent reading, but I found a way to reconcile my assigned stereotype with my passions. I microwaved nachos and ate them while reading Jackie Collins paperbacks I stole from my mother—trans fats, looting, *and* literature.

I chose to read *Sophie's Choice* as part of my English class's read-a-thon. The number of pages I read filled the classroom wall read-a-thon chart way before I was ready to admit that no nerd could catch up with me. I stole a piece of graph paper from math class and used a ruler to draw an extension for my row. I cut it out and stapled it to the bulletin board without asking my teacher's permission. I filled my annex with more book titles and more page numbers. I annexed that annex with another annex. I annexed that annex's annex with another annex and filled it. I wrote Anne Frank's name in there even though it was cheating. I read her in seventh grade. A whole year before.

Despite my intense bookwormery, my ho status eclipsed the rest of me. I gave in to the magnetic pull of other hos.

One of these hos, Janet (we'll say her last name was Jackson) was gifted with an ass that didn't match her ethnicity—a Swedish face with an Oakland booty. Her hobbies included abstract expressionism, oil painting, and the fight against cystic acne. I wanted to suggest to Janet that she combine these hobbies but kept this idea to myself. We hung out with a freckled undercover Mexican named Luna Smith. Luna's real last name had been Sanchez, but her dad legally changed it so the company he owned, Smith's Etc., wouldn't be associated with anything as foul as a Romance language.

It was lunchtime, and the three of us, plus Janet's skater lover, Bobby, were hanging out beneath untouchable monkey bars. We were too mature to dangle from them. We had body hair that required grooming.

Janet stood between two poles. Her pose reminded me of a cage dancer's in a music video. Bobby stood behind her, kneading her camel curves. Since her eyelashes were blond, it was sometimes hard to tell if they were there or what they were up to, but the way the sun was hitting them that afternoon, I could tell they were definitely fluttering. Low key, she was having an orgasm.

I squatted in the sand, watching popular girls walk the track. This was how they burned off the calories from the almond they split for lunch. Across the blacktop, by the fence separating us from the elementary school, bullies chased a dork into the pines. On his way past a retarded girl in a pantsuit, one bully screamed, "Nice tit!" Half the girl's chest swelled with a supremely developed breast. The other half of the girl's chest looked like mine.

I envied this girl's full boob but pitied her asymmetry. I prayed a Good Samaritan would teach her to stuff. That Good Samaritan would not be me.

Mamase Mamasa Mamakusa

A strand of Jheri curl uncoiled from under his fedora's brim and bounced above his surgical mask. His loafers made dainty sounds against the floor. He approached Pretzealot, our mall's pretzelry, each step exposing his white ankle socks.

In front of Pretzealot, a teen dressed as a pretzel held a tray of chopped-up pretzels. When he saw the celebrity, he forgot how ashamed of his costume he was. His tongs pinched a sample. He held it out.

The pretzel asked, "Pretzel?"

The singer shook his head. He clacked away from the baked good. He pedaled past the window display of a store selling Peruvian arts and crafts and owl figurines, Inca Hoots. He headed toward the dinging, glittering, and neon. A cave full of unsupervised children: the arcade. He was determined to taste what was there.

// //

Dad and four clerks colored at a round table in a government building. They used markers to vivify posters destined to help migrant kids, kids whose parents picked berries, beans, and other fruits, legumes, and vegetables. Dad's job was complicated and subsidized by Washington, but this part is easy to explain. He crafted teaching materials that went to classrooms where kids whose parents spoke Mixtec and/or Spanish could get their feet wet in English.

Apple.
Banana.
Cunt.
Durian.
Egg.
Father.
Girl.
Hoe.
Inchilada (very short enchilada)
Jheri curl.

Ku Klux Klan.

Leather daddy.

Mamase mamasa mamakusa.

Neverland.

One of the clerks, Noemi, was wearing an off-white sweater. She had a special-needs son, Felipe, who was named after his father. The elder Felipe worked as a gardener at Neverland Valley Ranch. The King of Pop employed lots of townsfolk since the ranch was so close, and we got pumped whenever he came into town to shop. Santa Maria had nothing special except for a ton of strawberries and a mall where a pop star sometimes came to cruise the toy store.

Noemi worked on a picture of a little boy, moving a yellow marker back and forth across his bangs. (When it sprouts from follicles, yellow turns blond. Blond can be sexy. Blond can be innocent. Blonds get to have more fun. Blonds get to embody duality. Brunettes don't get this privilege. Brunettes are doomed to ho and hoe.)

Noemi's Spanish accent slid a beast of burden into the name: Yakson. She explained that he'd invited the younger Felipe to the ranch for a sleepover.

Dad asked, "Are you going to let him go?"

Noemi smirked. She pushed up her sleeves and cocked her head to the side. Her accent turned her retort Semitic: "Mr. Gurba, are jew crazy?"

Dad and the clerks chortled.

They colored more.

Mormonse Mormonsa Mamakusa

I never entered the Osmonds' house, but from outside, it looked like it belonged on the East Coast. It looked stuffy yet cheerful. It was Ivy League and frat party at the same time. This was because of who lived and hung out there.

Mr. Osmond was a lawyer, a Mormon, and the dad. Though he had a daughter and a wife, boys played basketball in his driveway. Boys lounged in his backyard while he roasted Ball Park franks on the grill. His house was whitewashed and had red bricks and a chimney. No matter what time of year it was, at Mr. Osmond's, it was summer for boys.

I had PE with Mr. Osmond's son, Joey. For our uniform we had to wear a T-shirt and something under it. We got to choose what went under. We had to buy it from the sporting goods store, and we got a choice between green knee-length sweatpant shorts or booty shorts. Girls usually chose the booty shorts. Joey chose the booty shorts. They ended a hair past his cheeks and little slits nipped up his hips when he ambled. Joey's bowl cut moved how his butt moved in his shorts: swishily, but not in a gay way. Rumpelstiltskin had crafted Joey's hair color, and his eyes were backyard swimming pools that reminded us we were in California. The way he stared at girls made us aware that in his eyes, we skinny-dipped.

Joey bopped out of the locker room. Girls behind me whispered, "Joey has man legs."

It was true. Joey's leg's had pre matured.

Our PE teacher, Coach, glared at us as we formed "same-sex" lines along the blacktop. He screamed, "Bend and touch your toes!"

We Hitler Youthfully obeyed. We pressed our fingers into our shoes, which pressed against our toenails.

Coach screamed, "Grab your ankles!"

We held onto them. Our muscles woke up.

Coach yelled, "Let go, stand with your feet apart, and reach for the ground!"

This was the most humiliating pose. Perverts looked around to see what other people looked like in this pose so they would have something to masturbate to later on. I was curious about who was looking around. I glanced up. Joey was peeking around his knee and smiling. The spit on his braces sparkled.

"OK, good enough," growled Coach. "Walk it out, ladies."

Coach led us to the dirt track. In a loose herd, we waited. Coach put his whistle between his weathered lips. His cheeks swelled and the whistle screeched. Kids who took PE seriously took off like kids who take PE seriously. The rest of us jogged with the intensity of overcooked spaghetti.

Halfway through our lap, at the knoll shaded by stout pines, my lazy cohorts and I transitioned into a stroll. This was the polite thing to do. Kids who took PE seriously were assholes. They were going to get As but they were going to stink all day. None of them were going to take a shower. The showerheads in our locker room were pointless. They had as much use as the showerhead in Oświęcim. That's Polish for Auschwitz.

Assholes lapped us. We strolled the bend, heading toward the gym. I stretched. A yawn fluttered out of me.

"No way, ladies!" yelled Coach. "RUN!"

We sighed and jogged the dirt, quitting near the baseball dugout. That was a good quitting place. It was too far for Coach to yell at us.

I gazed to my left, through the chain-link fence that disappeared into an ice-plant-covered incline that gave way to a two-lane highway. A ditch gaped after the road, but it was too deep to see what was inside. Probably a fridge or a mattress with springs curling through the tears.

Buffalo approached. I sprang and flew into the grass. The others scattered too, and Joey and a bunch of Little Leaguers came sprinting through where we'd been. Their profiles showed excited teeth.

We saw their backs and their enviable calves. Their shoes pounded up the knoll, packing dirt, and Joey called, "Now!"

They hooked their thumbs into their waistbands and tugged their shorts down. Butts popped free. The humps hardly jiggled. They possessed the firmness of the newly ripened. Satisfied with getting some vitamin D, they let their shorts snap back up. The manliest boy, Tim, turned to look at us. He kissed the air.

As they sped away, we discussed their exposure. We evaluated what we'd seen. We mulled over how white they were, the strangeness of seeing ass in public, how one had hair on it, pretty much a coonskin cap, and I realized that this was the first time I'd ever been mooned.

Hammer

It was July, and Janet Jackson, the big-booty white girl I was friends with, had dumped her junior-high lover for someone new. This guy attended high school. He wore Hammer pants with a crotch that sagged to his knees. These were great for his job delivering pizzas. His nuts kept them warm.

Janet, her pizza boyfriend, and I were hanging out in Janet's kitchen while her parents were away at a Grateful Dead show. Janet leaned against the counter, making it easier for him to touch her. Though the counter obscured them both from the waist down, I knew she was getting touched where it counted.

I stood barefoot by the fridge, humming Queensrÿche's "Silent Lucidity." I held a bottle of alcohol in each hand. Together they represented my ancestry.

The pizza boyfriend narrowed his eyes at me. "What are you?" he asked.

I looked at the tequila. "Mexican," I slurred.

He reared his head back. Cocked it. Narrowed his eyes at me so that his suspicion could not be ignored. "But you have green eyes," he said. "You can't be all bean."

Since I had swigged from both bottles, I didn't have the lucidity to explain my eye color. I didn't have it in me to argue that I got my green eyes from my dad, who got his green eyes from his mom, a mean-ass Mexican who thinks she's better than all the other Mexicans because of her eye color—a color he believes doesn't belong to us.

I looked at the vodka. "I'm a quarter Polish," I added.

The pizza boyfriend grinned. He declared, "The two stupidest races ever. Combined!"

// //

JANICE DICKINSON FRÉDÉRIC CHOPIN JOSEPH CONRAD JOHN WAYNE GACY MARIE CURIE PIA ZADORA SAM WAGSTAFF LEON CZOLGOSZ TADEUSZ KOŚCIUSZKO POPE JOHN PAUL II CHLOË SEVIGNY and TED KACZYNSKI are all Polish. Richard Ramirez Speedy Gonzales Selena Jennifer Lopez Menudo Dora the Explorer and ALF are not. Of all of Eddie Van Halen's wives, Valerie Bertinelli looks the most Polish Mexican.

Bonnie

My junior-high friends went to the public high school across the street from the Catholic one my parents sent me to.

I got a fresh batch of friends there. Not all of them were hos. Some were drunks and fools. One new friend loved high fashion and was half black and half Spanish. Her name was Conchita. She said *Barthelona*. Conchita and my other new friends were the kinds of girls whose best years wouldn't be in high school. They were also the kinds of girls whose senior superlatives were things like Best Chin. One of them, Frida, was half Mexican. That attracted me to her.

The whitest among my new friends was Ashley. Ashley had blond hair and no lips. She wore cowboy boots without irony. She believed in her beauty and told us that when she was having sex with Steve Panini, he told her she looked like Alicia Silverstone, the girl from *Clueless* who also played Lolita. After giving Ashley this compliment, Steve ate her ass. I wondered how it tasted. I wondered how clean she kept it. Her self-esteem floored me.

Ashley's belief in herself and her beauty made watching her sophomore year trauma painful. She hit us all up for money to enter a beauty pageant, flew to Las Vegas, and competed. She ignored Frida's advice: "Fuck a judge."

Ashley placed last, so when it was announced that Miss America was coming to our school as part of her post-coronation tour, Ashley wasn't into it. We were sitting behind a religion classroom and Ashley yelled, "Fuck Miss America!"

"Keep yellin' it!" yelled Frida. "It's not like she can hear you."

It was around noon. We sat on a concrete curb that hemmed acacias. For lunch, Ashley was dipping tobacco. Frida was eating tuna on whole wheat. Conchita was spooning paella. I was watching.

In imitation deaf-voice, Ashley groaned, "NYOO AH BOOTIFUL!"

You are beautiful.

I shivered. Ashley's cruelty gave me goose bumps.

Our soon-to-be-arriving Miss America's thing was that she was hard of hearing. Our school had been scrubbed and groomed for her afternoon visit. The male teachers were wearing ties and deodorant in anticipation of her. Ashley wanted to slash her face. She wanted to smash it with a rock till it bled marinara.

"That bitch," said Ashley. "That bitch is going to give us some bullshit talk she can't even hear."

We nodded to show Ashley that we believed deaf Miss America had cunt breath. That's what you do when you're in high school and someone is your friend. You agree that other girls are cunts to prove your fealty to the girls you love.

"Let's ditch," said Ashley. "Let's get the fuck out of here."

"Yeah," giggled Frida. "Let's leave!"

Frida and Ashley looked at Conchita. She said, "I don't care what we do as long as I can smoke." She was so European.

"How are we gonna do it?" I asked. "We're locked in."

Ashley looked down the breezeway, at the tall chain-link fence bordering the parking lot. "We'll hop the fence by the chapel," she said. "My car's over there."

"I'm not good at climbing fences," I said.

Ashley said, "We'll help you. Just be there instead of the assembly. Don't pussy out."

"Yeah!" cried Frida. She shook her tuna fish sandwich so that the pieces of bread moved like lips. "Don't pussy out!" she bellowed. I think she was trying to do some sort of vaginal ventriloquism.

// //

I flattened myself against the chapel wall. Frida and Conchita were on either side of me, also flattened.

Ashley tossed her wool-lined jacket so it draped over the wires twisting along the top of the fence. It was cool that she was sacrificing it so that our hands and crotches would be protected. We were going to thank her by climbing over the jacket, running away from school, and saying mean things about Miss America.

Ashley lunged at the fence and grabbed. She inserted one cowboy-boot toe into a chain-link slot and scuttled. Disobedience made her glow. It was better than makeup.

Reaching her jacket, Ashley lifted her leg. She straddled the fence, hoisted her other leg over, and let go. She was an angel falling five or six feet and landing with bent knees; she needed no time to collect herself. She sprinted off to go warm up her Scirocco.

I felt bad but good bad. I felt slightly criminal. Instead of Bonnie and Clyde, we were all Bonnie.

Conchita mimicked Ashley going over and made it to the car. Frida went over quickly for someone with basketball tits and joined the others in the car. I sighed and stepped up to the fence. I looked down. The last thing on the mind of the homosexual who'd invented platform Mary Janes was rappelling out of Catholic school, but I was going to have to summon the skill to make it happen.

I grabbed a handful of fence. I inserted my shoe. My toe fit perfectly into the square hole. My morale grew. I moved my feet and my hands sailed. I realized I actually could be athletic as long as I was doing it for all the wrong reasons. I reached the jacket in less than thirty seconds. I straddled it and felt the fence undulate.

My fingers let go. I dropped to the cement. My platforms touched down. My chest felt chilly because half of my outfit was still on the fence.

On my way down, wire had stabbed my black blouse and ripped it off. It waved in the wind like a pirate flag. I glanced at the ground. Black buttons lay scattered across the cement. They reminded me of Frosty the Snowman's eyes. I looked up. I reached for my blouse and tore it free. I grabbed Ashley's jacket too. Turning, I ran to the Scirocco. It was either going to die or take us somewhere less shitty.

// //

Conchita undid the safety pins in her skirt. She slid them out of the hem, and I turned and presented my back to her. I felt her yanking, stabbing them into the fabric, pinning me shut again.

// //

Ashley's right foot pushed the gas pedal. Her left foot hung out the window. It was riding doggy style. It was practically smiling.

// //

The thing I hate most about riding in the backseat when two smokers are in front is seeing embers come at my eyes. It makes blinking crucial.

// //

Conchita sucked herb through a yellow, green, and red pipe. I sucked a lollipop. All the windows were rolled down. The sound of wind made it hard to talk. Wind played with our hair. It whipped our cheeks, but it didn't feel punishing.

// //

While Ashley hit the pipe, her right elbow steered.

Bushes hid a highway patrolman parked in a Mustang. He ignored us. We weren't worth coming out of the bush for.

We crossed a bridge that spanned a riverbed-turned-desert. Tumbleweeds and sand filled it.

We ignored how tall the pines were growing at the Christmas tree farm next to the trailer park we sped past. Nobody commented on the Pacific Ocean sparkling to our left. It was just another swimming pool, and those are everywhere in California. California wants everyone to take her top off and jump in.

// //

We passed strawberry fields.

Mexicans hunched in them, harvesting. These were the Mexicans whose kids Dad made educational materials for, and there I was, riding up the freeway with drugs, multicultural friends, and candy. I felt bad that I was mostly Mexican but didn't have to be out there doing that, ruining my body so people could have strawberries to eat. Adrenaline and other chemicals overwhelmed my guilt. Adrenaline and female bonding can overwhelm almost anything.

I stared at the Mexicans.

I sucked on my lollipop.

// //

We got off the freeway in San Luis Obispo.

San Luis is a town famous for a hotel named the Madonna Inn. It has nothing to do with Madonna. It's also got a college that satirical musician "Weird Al" Yankovic attended and a nearby penal colony that housed a member of the Manson Family.

We parked in front of a café, a place where college kids congregated to drink coffee and feel superior to those who didn't share their worldviews. Conchita fed the parking meter. She announced, "That's it. That's the last of my McDonald's money." After school, Conchita cooked quarter pounders with cheese and looked chic doing it.

"Let's beg," I suggested.

We left the Scirocco and trudged toward the sawhorses blocking the main street. A farmers' market was underway there and this was something to see and do. Yeah, people were selling fruits, vegetables, and nuts, but people were also stirring vats of popcorn, and politically minded assholes were registering voters at folding tables. You could buy a sunflower as tall as you once were. We didn't have this back home, just deaf Miss America, so we were going to enjoy it. We needed more money to enjoy it.

Frida and I paired off. We walked. We passed a lady with a face-painting booth and a person begging people to sign his petition to save something. I directed Frida to a window display where pale mannequins created soft-core porn dioramas. This store was Fanny Wrappers. It sold intimate apparel. Statues dressed in lace teddies and thongs beckoned at passersby. Some pedestrians stared and blushed, and others pretended like there weren't pretend women wearing real lingerie right in front of them. Across the street from us, Ashley and Conchita loitered in front of a less, or maybe more, erotic window display: leather shoes.

A blond bowl cut bobbed through the river of local vegetables, steam, and petals. Frida whispered, "There goes Joey Osmond. His dad got to third base with the entire Little League."

She was exaggerating. He'd gotten to third base with the kids he'd coached. We knew because it'd been on the news that Mr. Osmond was chomo: that's shorthand for a child-molesting homosexual. He'd finagled the jizz out of the kids he taught baseball to and probably the kids he represented pro bono in the juvenile court system. Interestingly, he taught Sunday school. I wondered if his lessons on Sodom and Gomorrah had been interactive.

The news said his church had known what he was up to for a while because boys had told on him, but instead of kicking him out, his bishop had gotten him therapy. This cured him and made it OK to put him among boys again. Everyone in town found the news about the Osmonds titillating because the Osmonds were considered a whole-grain breakfast-cereal type of family—crisp, nourishing, and unostentatious—but this was revealed as a lie.

The Little League boys Mr. Osmond touched testified against him and wept in the witness box. They were boys I went to junior high with, boys who had mooned me, one who had stuck his hand in my pudding, who had pressed on my clit in class. If molestation is a circle, a circle of life, then isn't the hand of every molester working through the hand of every other molester? It's fair to say that Mr. Osmond's hand was working through Macaulay's hand just like the Eucharist is no longer bread during Mass; it's Jesus coming at you through a cracker.

My heart refused to have compassion for those involved in our local chomo mess. Compassion was too risky.

"I'm sure he made it to home base with some of them," I said to Frida. "I mean, he had, like, foster kids and foreign exchange students staying at his house all the time. He created a potlatch."

A hippie with pube-ish sideburns oozed by.

"Give us money," I told him.

"For what?" he asked.

"We might buy food with it or we might get high. It depends."

The hippie reached into his overalls pocket and removed a Guatemalan textile wallet. He pulled beauty from it, a twenty-dollar bill. He lifted it into the air above his blond 'fro.

"If you want it," he said, "come and get it."

Feeling like a hooker, I leapt, snatched the money, and petted it.

"Thank him," said Frida.

"Thanks a lot, dick," I said.

The hippie's eyes bugged.

"That's no way to show appreciation!" Frida screamed theatrically. "Blow the man!" she commanded.

"Nope," I said. "I'm homo."

"Homo schlomo," she replied. "You can still blow the man!"

The hippie sized me up from platforms to bangs. "You seem pretty young to have decided what team to bat for," he said.

Frida and I looked at Joey Osmond; he was languishing with his back to a lotion shop, watching a clown. The clown's yarn hair hung with tragic limpness. He juggled worn and tarnished balls without enthusiasm. Joey looked away from the balls. He frowned.

Frida put her arm around me. I felt her big breast press my bicep.

"They start pretty young these days," Frida said. The hippie smirked, but his smirk didn't matter. His smirk couldn't touch us. Only we could touch each other.

Via Dolorosa

Thanks to Mr. Osmond, our neighborhood was no longer tranquil. It was, however, still gorgeous.

My sister, Ofelia, was trying to be gorgeous.

As a premenstrual girl, she'd been soft, round, and sensitive. Like, hearing Dad call Mom a bitch could make her cry. The dying tweets of a bird trapped in Dad's car engine made her weep. Having her arms pinned behind her back by an asshole while neighborhood boys jumped our brother made her hysterical. (Kids shoved, kicked, and punched Herman because he wore glasses, did his homework, and founded the chess club. He was brown, gangly, and not mean enough to be cool. He wasn't a sissy, but everyone could still tell.)

My parents' intent in making Ofelia and Herman was to give me a playmate. They didn't. They created a set of creatures that existed for each other.

That's how twins work; they're an island unto themselves. Anyone with twins as siblings knows this. Herman and Ofelia spoke to each other with silence. Sitting beside them, I could feel them having telepathic exchanges. Through our living room windows, I watched them silently hunt for specimens for Herman's bug collection.

They got to go to junior high together, and I envied that. It's good to have someone, especially someone you can communicate with preternaturally, present during the weirdest time of your life. Seventh grade can be that time.

Herman went to tang soo do classes after school. At the dojo, he learned to chop. Ofelia went to ballet. At the dance studio, she learned that she ought to unleash her bones. Her mealtime behavior turned strange. I stared at her in the dining room. Its terrible wallpaper featured watercolor oranges dangling from long, turd-like branches. Oranges play a sacred role in the history of female starvation. Legend has it that every Friday, Saint Veronica, female starvation's patron saint, ate five orange seeds to commemorate Christ's five wounds. Vitamin C.

At dinner, Ofelia hunched beneath our hexagonal wall clock. Her hazel eyes stared at proteins, carbs, and fats. She poked them with forks, spoons, knives, and fingers. She stirred sour cream and beans in figure eights. She minced scrambled eggs to dust. She spread her mashed potatoes and smashed green beans into them, making and remaking mounds. Her thin lips remained clamped. It was a hearty meal if she ate an entire scoop of canned corn.

Our parents stared at her and fidgeted. They furrowed their brows and sighed. They pursed their lips with frustration. I silently prayed to a god I didn't believe in, asking him to intervene and fix the situation. I tried to set a big-sisterly example by eating all my food, even the food I hated.

I swallowed all my lima beans.

"Eat your food," Dad told her. "Don't play with it. One time my sister wouldn't eat her eggs, and my father smashed her face right into them. She stopped fooling around after that."

I'd seen enough after-school specials and read enough young-adult fiction to understand what was happening. In Mom and Dad's room, I told Mom, "Ofelia has anorexia."

The corners of her lips turned down. The long creases made her look equal parts worried and sad. She shook her head. In Spanish, she said, "I don't think so. She just needs to eat more."

When I made the same announcement to Dad, he shook his head even more vigorously. He said, "I don't think so. She just needs to stop playing with her food."

Once Ofelia's leotards fit her loosely, Mom made an appointment with our pediatrician. I came along. Dr. Hamilton's office smelled like glass, steel, and immunity, how I imagined it smelled inside a syringe. He'd inherited the practice from his father, a white Nevisian who'd had a stroke. I preferred the older Dr. Hamilton. He always smiled and complimented the girth of my earlobes. "Great for jewelry," he'd say. Young Dr. Hamilton said nothing about my earlobes. He parted his hair down the middle. He wore corduroy. He exuded confidence and inexperience, a combination that gave me pause.

"Stand on the scale," he told Ofelia.

She stepped onto it. He fingered the scale's black square. He peered at the number it framed.

"Eighty pounds," he muttered. He recorded her weight on her chart.

Mom stood across from him next to the examination table. A straw purse covered in hot-pink roses dangled from her forearm. Square glasses shielded half her face. She sputtered, "Ofelia doesn't eat. It's very hard for us to get her to eat." Her voice cracked, a sign that she was going to cry. I watched a tear fall and cut through her blush. "Could she have anorexia?" asked Mom.

I was proud of Mom for saying the word. I was relieved she was crying. I believed her tears would get her taken seriously.

Dr. Hamilton chuckled. He said, "She isn't anorexic. She can't be."

"Why?" asked Mom.

"You're Mexican," he answered.

He filled out a prescription and tore it off his pad. He handed it to Mom.

I peeked at it. His handwriting was appropriately terrible.

Mom stared at the paper. Through sniffles, she asked, "What does this say?"

Dr. Hamilton answered, "Make her eat double."

He smiled. It wasn't every day that such a pretty and confused Mexican lady cried in his office.

I left his office feeling he'd sentenced Ofelia to die.

// //

UMILIANA DE' CERCHI MARGHERITA DA CORTONA CATERINA DA SIENA ANGELA DA FOLIGNO COLOMBA DA RIETI VERONICA DE' JULIANIS MARIE D'OIGNIES BEATRIJS VAN NAZARETH and JULIAN OF NORWICH spoke a lean and ancient language. OFELIA OF SANTA MARIA spoke it, too. Female fasting has its own grammar and syntax. Men, especially fathers, often misinterpret it. By fasting, a girl ascends a throne made of bone. She stares into the face of the divine and beyond. She finds that infinity has no caloric value. This is fine. Emptiness comes to nourish her. It replaces her marrow. All of her hope calcifies, cracks, and disappears. She laughs at gravity.

// //

Ofelia got as wispy and quiet as a ghost.

Everything became baggy on her, and my parents finally relented. Mom drove her to see a Harvard-educated psychiatrist in Santa Barbara. I came along.

While Ofelia and Mom did whatever they did behind the shrink's office door, I sat, legs crossed, on the waiting room's Scandinavian furniture. Nothing hung from the smooth ecru walls. Even the light bulbs seemed expensive. The posh minimalism gave me hope. Somebody with this much taste had to be able to cure my sister. Mozart played softly. There was a stack of *New Yorkers* splayed on the end table.

I reached for a magazine, opened it, and admired its fonts. I held it up to my face so that my nose touched a poem. I sniffed.

"So this is what mental health smells like . . . " I thought. It wasn't cheap. It certainly wasn't Mexican.

// //

The lower the glucose, the closer to . . .

// //

I knew the stories of Ofelia's spiritual antecedents.

I read about them in books I kept in my bedroom. Their stories are fed to Catholic girls as exemplars of good girlhood. Good girlishness resists gluttony. Good girlishness resists pleasure. Good girls prove their virtue by getting rid of themselves. Saint Catherine did this by eating only herbs and Eucharist. Mystic pizza. When she was force-fed, like I watched my parents try to do to Ofelia, she shoved twigs down her throat to barf up the unwanted items. Saint Angela survived on a diet of air, scabs, and lice. For drink, she sucked leaky wounds. Mary of Oignies thanked Jesus whenever her throat swelled shut at the sight of food. Emaciation saved Blessed Columba. Would-be rapists peeked under her dress, and her bones so turned them off that they spared her. She went on to starve her way past Saint Peter. Death by anorexia is a fail-safe sexual-assault prevention technique.

I was pretty sure Ofelia hadn't eaten anything in three days when Dad dropped us off at the movies. I bought our tickets, a bag of popcorn, and a Sprite. We sat in the second row. *The Nightmare Before Christmas* played. An extra-large T-shirt hid Ofelia, but I was certain that underneath it she looked like Jack, the skeleton who was the animated movie's hero. Good guys tend to be thin, white, and melodious.

Movie light illuminated Ofelia's face. It traced her hollowness and turned her beatific.

Her curly mane was pulled into a tight ponytail that sprouted from the back of her skull. Escaped frizz caught in the movie light gave her a halo. She looked the part. She looked pious, medieval, and ready for martyrdom. Saint Veronica would have been proud. I watched her hand dip into the popcorn bag. Each time it exited, it carried a solitary piece of popcorn. She placed these on her tongue.

I glanced at her to see if she chewed. She didn't. She seemed to let each kernel melt. She swallowed imperceptibly.

In those moments that Ofelia was able to break her fast long enough to enjoy the decadence of movie popcorn, she transfixed me. I believed that she loved me. She loved me enough to break her taboo with me. I felt honored.

It honored me that she chose to eat with me.

Her illness made me understand the meaning of female sovereignty. Ofelia deserved to be bathed in light.

// //

When Ofelia went to live at the hospital, she became even more of a ghost.

You could see her in Dad's scowl and in Mom's pallor. You could feel her around Herman, as if her skeletal spirit stood behind him, peeking at you from behind his martial arts uniform.

Her absence was haunting the house, and I didn't want to be there. I ran away from her ghost.

I started weekending at Frida's.

Frida lived in a one-story house by the fairgrounds. Her mom, Ester, worked as a hairdresser and spoke with an accent like Mom's. That comforted me. Ester didn't bug us about what we did Friday and Saturday nights and that endeared her to me, too.

Frida's bedroom walls were gray, and the words *joker, smoker,* and *midnight toker* were painted in black above her bed. Those three things described Frida. So did *official.* She served as our school's Students Against Drunk Driving vice president. Ashley was president.

Ashley and Frida loved to drink. Who doesn't?

I love drinking. Till I don't.

Ashley, Frida, Conchita, and I drank at the beach, in cars, and out of cans. We drank with boys, girls, and neither. I loved drinking with people I knew or wanted to know, and I even liked drinking with people I couldn't stand. I liked the way my mouth tasted when I drank. I liked the way other people's mouths tasted when they drank.

Ashley insisted she drove better while drunk, and she was drunk when she drove us to the park to meet some boys. We parked on the street and walked to the bleachers. We sat on them, guzzled beer and malt liquor, and threw our cans and bottles at the outfield. I was feeling buzzed when a squad car pulled toward us. Its tires crushed the lawn. Headlights cut through the dark, tracing blades of grass, bleachers, then us.

The car stopped. The cop got out. He paced toward us. I stared at his baton.

"What are you doing here?" he asked.

"Waiting for friends," answered Ashley. She flipped her blond hair over her shoulder. It would save us. Its color purged us of sin, conferred innocence on our group.

"The park is closed," said the cop. "Leave."

"OK," said Ashley. We staggered after her, to the Scirocco.

The cop's uniformed silhouette watched us pull away. We drove cackling into the night.

// //

You never know what spaces might turn into graves. It felt bad—OK, sickening—when I realized I'd partied on her grave, but you just never know if you're standing on a spot where someone has been or will be beaten to death. It's cheesy, but sometimes my concerns about the history of violence taint everything, even Shakespeare. That quote "All the world's a stage" becomes "All the world's a grave."

I tossed empty bottles on her grave before it became her grave. I was allowed to escape. I was allowed to walk away from that spot.

Sophia was not. Guilt is a ghost. Guilt interrupts narratives. It does so impolitely. Ghosts have no etiquette. What do they need it for? There is no Emily Post for ghosts.

// //

Buzzed, Ashley drove us from the park to Lyon's.

This diner stood across the street from the Santa Maria Inn, a hotel where Valentino once stayed. We crowded into a corner banquette. We peered at our waitress through the secondhand smoke.

Lindsay, this Mormon girl who sometimes hung out with us, declared, "Hi, Elizabeth!" through the haze.

Our waitress smiled through her annoyance. "Hi," she said. "Are you guys actually gonna order something?"

I kind of knew Elizabeth from the parties we went to. She'd be at them looking skinny, pretty, and Mexican. She was a bobblehead Mexican, the kind that are so skinny you worry their heads will fall off if they get excited. I didn't know much about Elizabeth other than that boys were really into her and wanted to have sex with her. I didn't get it. She seemed so frail and brittle that I imagined rubbing up against her for a long time might be like rubbing against kindling: a fire hazard. She naturally had the kind of body Ofelia had almost killed herself to achieve. (Ofelia was home again. Her weight had been brought up through nasogastric tube feeding.)

"What are you insinuating?" Frida snapped.

"That you guys never order anything."

"Well," said Frida, "we're gonna have onion rings and *two* bowls of ranch. And . . . another ashtray."

Elizabeth made a face like we were worthless bitches and turned to walk away. Her apron flipped up as she did.

I put my head down on the table and breathed in secondhand smoke. It encased me amniotically.

Something I Often Reflect on as an Adult Woman

I still have unserved detentions.

The Unbearable Whiteness of Certain Girls

I listened to Billie Holiday on certain school nights. With my underwear soaked in period blood, I crawled across my bedroom carpet. I got intimate with it. I knelt at the stereo. A cassette spun on the tape deck. Blues filled the corner. I fell to my side and curled my body around an invisible ball of feelings that was tethered to me as if by an umbilical cord.

A pretty heroin addict from long ago was singing to me.

She was voicing how it felt to be in love.

She was voicing how it felt for me to be in love with a white girl.

"You're my thrill. You do something to me. You send chills right through me. When I look at you. 'Cause you're my thrill . . ."

"You're My Thrill" expressed every emotion I felt for this white girl, and it didn't matter that a whole bunch of time and space existed between me and Billie Holiday. Her delivery proved to me that she understood how crazy in love I was with this girl I'm not even going to bother describing. All the white girls I fall for are the same. They're all Michelle Pfeiffer. Or James Dean. None of them have been Nina Simone. None of them have been Richard Pryor. None of them have been Screamin' Jay Hawkins. Only Billie Holiday could voice my yearning. She was dead. That seemed fitting.

This white girl who I french-kissed went to Catholic school with me. She kept her things in a locker by the chapel. The pimple on her chin turned me on. Every part of her turned me on. We touched titties and tongues in her bedroom. We bit each other. Her hands bruised my arms and flanks and we tasted one another's blood. We crawled through moonlight into dark, wet tunnels and felt each other's necks. She listened to Zeppelin. She had her flaws.

I enjoy saying that my father forcing me to mow the lawn and use the leaf blower turned me gay. I also blame MTV's *The Real World*. Do you even know what *The Real World* was? It was reality. It was a TV show where a bunch of fairly good-looking people with conflicting identity politics were put together in a house, plied with free alcohol, and filmed giving one another lectures and HPV.

The San Francisco season premiered at the same time I invited the white girl of my dreams over for enchiladas. Pedro starred as the gay cast member. That was a thing in the nineties—the gay cast member.

Like me, Pedro wasn't white. He was light skinned but not white; there's a difference. Pedro dated a black guy. He had a handsome face and spoke with a Cuban accent. When had a Cuban on TV last been so popular? It had to have been Ricky Ricardo. Pedro was dying of AIDS. He was doing it better than Magic Johnson.

Pedro had beef with one of his roommates, Puck. Puck was a white guy of the worst type: a white guy with a bicycle. He delivered things on his bike. He was a bike messenger. He reveled in being disgusting in a very "boys will be boys" kind of way, and the show's editors dedicated a segment to his grossness. They juxtaposed this grossness against Pedro's AIDS-y gentility.

A scene opens with Pedro being interviewed. In an accent similar to Mom's, he says, "I really have a big problem with Puck. I'm fixing myself a bagel with peanut butter and I'm getting really into it." Cut to Pedro in the kitchen. Sensual R & B plays as he slices a bagel. The musical choice suggests that gay Latinos sexually interact with everything. Sticking a knife into a bagel is erotic for us.

We don't see the fingering happen, but we see Puck walking out of the kitchen, seemingly chewing, and over his shoulder Pedro calls, "Did you stick your finger in the peanut butter?" Cut back to the interview, where Pedro confirms that yes, Puck stuck his finger up his nose and then fingered the peanut butter jar, licked his digit, and went on with his straight life.

Puck denies his crime. The tapes are replayed. They vindicate Pedro. Puck totally did it.

Watching this drama made me hungry for a bagel. It also made me wonder if Pedro ever got so frustrated he wished he could give Puck AIDS.

// //

In college, I met a conservative gay writer with HIV.

He was dating the roommate of this boy I was having experimental sex with, and once he walked into their sparely furnished living room while I was hanging out on the couch in sweats and radiating viral heat.

My immune system was fighting something fluey. I could feel coughs growing inside me.

The writer strode toward me. I remained seated. He reached out his hand and said, "Hello, I'm Andrew."

"Hello," I replied to the Englishman I already knew to be Andrew Sullivan. "I'm sick."

In a tiny way, I felt powerful. Powerful enough to kill Andrew Sullivan by coughing on him.

Andrew Sullivan made a yikes face.

He waved at me in place of a handshake and paced to the balcony. There, his date, a gorgeous white boy, was waiting, leaning against the railing. Andrew Sullivan put his hands around the swimmer's shoulders. He pressed his chest against the boy's back, HIV positive to HIV negative.

// //

Pedro's accent soothed me. His beauty soothed me. The high stakes of his life so inspired me, they almost made me want to have AIDS. But I think being in love with a mean white girl was enough. She was my AIDS.

// //

The Real World: San Francisco had a gay. *The Real World: Los Angeles* had a lesbian. The roommates found out when she wore her "I'm Not Gay But My Girlfriend Is" T-shirt to shoot pool.

// //

Pedro partly made me come out to Mom.

If he could argue with a bike messenger on international TV about sticking his finger in peanut butter, the least I could do was acknowledge that I was bonkers for a white girl.

Scarlett O'Hara, Lana Turner, Divine. White girls.

Baltimore drag queens make the prettiest white girls.

// //

White girls are the Holy Grails of Western civilization. I wish they could be replaced with something else. Let there be a new grail. Let that grail be a dead Mexican woman in a long dress. Let her name be Wisdom.

Let her ghost unmoor the hero's journey. Let the ghost whisper her sibilant name. Let her breathe it right into your mouth.

// //

I still hang out with white girls. I still hang out with ghosts.

// //

When do you think white girls will go extinct? We are more than a decade into the twenty-first century, and I see no indications of their decline.

There are still plenty of them to feel inferior to.

There are still plenty of them to get high with.

The last one I hung out with hates men.

She lives with her partner on a street with a funny name. Something like Cerulean or Imbroglio.

The white girl delivers marijuana. Unlike Puck, she uses a Honda. One of her clients is a high school teacher who invites her to sit at her kitchen table. The teacher will pack a bowl and ply the white girl with weed, peppering her with questions about transgendered womanhood. Since the white girl is kind of new to her job, she feels like she has to humor the teacher. She can't stand it, though. She's not a teacher. The teacher is.

The white girl and I are pharmaceutical sisters. I take estradiol twice a day and progesterone once a day to supplement my failing ovaries. I take spironolactone to fix the mess my adrenal glands make. The white girl takes these same hormones and androgen blockers for other reasons. Mainly, it's because her ovaries exist on an alternate level of consciousness. She's trans.

We squatted on her tiny stoop together. The night sky gave us a whole bunch of black to stare at. Her cat pranced along the lawn. With cautious paws, she crept toward my feet. She crouched as if she were going to come at me and then leapt back and darted into the grass.

Her tail twitched. Its tip seemed to have been hacked off and then peeled. "What happened to her tail?" I asked.

The white girl said, "Bob accidentally slammed the door on it and she tried to yank it out and ripped the fur off. When Bob opened the door, it was just bones and blood. He felt so bad." The white girl shook her head. Her strawberry-blond curls bounced.

She crossed her legs and tugged her miniskirt toward her knees. "We had to put a cone on her because she kept chewing it. It's healing now. It looks way better."

We stared at the cat. I wondered what the raw tail would have tasted like. I considered the default: chicken.

The cat twitched her nub.

The white girl asked, "Want some?" She held out a smoldering J.

"No thanks."

The cat frolicked. The white girl asked, "Do you like acid?"

"I've never done it," I said.

"Oh, I love it," she said. She scrunched her curls and sang acid's praises. It was her favorite.

After she finished telling me about some trip she went on using experimental drugs, I told her, "One time, in junior high, this boy gave me a tab. Since it was wrapped in foil I thought it looked like jewelry, so I kept it in my jewelry box. That way my parents couldn't find it. It just blended in."

The white girl reached for her curls. She scrunched. "Coke makes me so horny," she said. "I love coke."

We wandered back inside her house. The soft recessed lighting made me feel like we were in a peach. I was sitting on the carpet, hating my body. To my right, a huge flat-screen played a music video. White girls in swimsuits ran on a beach, showing off their peaches. The white girl's endless legs hung off the couch. Her fingers curled. Purple acrylics scratched her thigh, tattooed with the word *misandry* to express her hatred for the male sex.

This tattooed thigh makes her the ultimate woman.

Baby rocks tumbled from a plastic sack that she tipped over her phone. They hit the screen and she set the phone down on the glass-topped coffee table. Swiping, she pressed a Costco membership card to the rocks, flattened them, and made little white beaches. She raked the plastic across them and chopped.

She snatched a dollar bill off a closed laptop and rolled it into a tight tunnel. Leaning over, she placed the money between her nostril and the whiteness then dragged it along the beach. The beach vanished.

Crack

Ida, the white girl who smoked crack on accident, was back.

We got separated by the medieval period known as junior high, but her mom sent her to Catholic school even though they were Lutheran. We had most of our classes together. Any time we could, we sat next to each other. Our teachers yelled at us for talking to each other too much, and when we got home from school, we sprinted to our phones so we could call each other and keep talking. I slept over at her house even more than I slept at Frida's. That's what you do when you love someone a lot. You spend time unconscious with them.

We held hands under Ida's covers. Her sheets smelled hellish because her water came from a sulfurous well. She, her mom, and her stepdad lived in a canyon that the city water didn't reach—you had to drive over several dirt roads to get there. Wild turkeys loitered in these roads. Mountain lions and rattlesnakes frolicked amid the surrounding oaks. Spanish moss hung from the branches.

Ida's stepdad, Ralph, was such a white guy. He sat on a rocking chair on their front porch, wearing flannel, mom jeans, and trucker hats. He chewed tobacco and occasionally let the juice spill onto his Santa beard. His cheeks glowed merrily. He kept a rifle nearby.

Glancing at him from behind the living room's white lace curtains, I knew I would be the perfect thing for him to kill. That's what men who looked like him did in the olden days in California: they killed Mexicans. They lynched us. Made us into strange fruit. Mangos, maybe. My death would've made Ralph a better white man in California's past.

My death would've made Ralph a better white man in California's present.

Ralph loved whiteness. When we weren't around, he sniffed it up his nose and revved his truck. He barreled out of the canyon and into town to hammer buildings together. At the moment, he was resting. Thinking. Staring at the lawn, which was strange. A savage hill and then suddenly, civilization. A house and a lawn.

Sun-bleached Weimaraner shit speckled the grass. I scanned the green for reptiles. When rattlesnakes slithered onto it to tan themselves, Ralph would take care of them. He'd reach for his rifle, aim, and shoot. I never saw him do it, but Ida explained: "When the bullets hit them, their bodies look like exploding ropes."

// //

Ida could be a dumb bitch sometimes.

Like during the fifth-grade race war, as I was lamenting getting called a beaner and a wetback, she said, "I know how you feel."

I squinted at her.

"How?" I asked.

She pointed at her head. "I'm blond," she answered. She got teary-eyed. "I'm sick of the jokes."

I rolled my eyes and said a silent prayer for every blond Mexican.

The phone was ringing. It was Sunday. Maybe Ida was calling to tell me something dumb. Like that reverse racism is real.

"Hello?"

Crazed sobbing. The only other time I heard a girl cry like that was when Tupac got shot.

"Ida?" I said.

Weird syllables broke through the sobs. Maybe Ida's stepdad had accidentally shot her mom. Maybe she'd found out Santa wasn't real.

"Ida!" I demanded. "What happened?"

"His dogs," she choked. "They got Golem!"

She resumed sobbing.

The news was so horrific I had to stifle laughter. Golem was the love of Ida's life, a black cat that slept on her face and tried to sleep on mine. She talked to him almost as much as she talked to me, and now her step-dad's hunting dogs had assassinated him. I imagined them getting into his drugs and making a coked-out sport of cat shredding.

"I'm not coming to school tomorrow!" she cried. I heard a click.

Memories of every mean thing I'd ever done to Ida returned. Freshman year, when she forgot her grammar and composition book in her locker, she'd call me so I could dictate the sentences we were supposed to diagram. I'd made up extra ones for her. I laughed along with her brother when he teased her and intimated she had sexual relations with her cat. When she called me crying to share the score she'd gotten on the Advanced Placement Language and Composition exam, a two, and asked what I'd gotten, I answered honestly: "A five."

Was it an act of meanness to admit that I'd gotten a perfect score, especially when one of my parents wasn't even a native speaker of the language?

Maybe.

Monday, at school, Ida's chair remained empty.

In religion class, I tuned out a lecture about miracles and lepers. I slouched behind my Bible, which was propped upright on my desk. I skimmed *The Communist Manifesto,* which I'd wedged into the Gospels. Vague as it was, I still preferred Marx's alms-for-everyone utopia to the snow-white heaven we got snapshots of in class. White is so hard to keep clean.

I looked at Ida's empty seat and imagined her heaven: No sex. Plenty of cats. I contrasted hers with mine: No cats. Plenty of sex. This day-dream fused with Marxist theory and I succumbed to fantasies of feline free love, an orgy of proletariat meow, which ended with the sound of the lunch bell.

// //

"My mom keeps telling me it's OK if I'm gay, but I'm not gay." Ida spoke from the corner where she knelt shoving sneakers into a pile. Softening her voice, she added, "I think I'm asexual."

"Tell her that," I said.

"I did, but she keeps pushing."

"I like girls."

Ida flinched a little—my lesbianism hurt her. She'd recently fallen in love with Jesus and had been spending a lot of time with him.

Ida's mom was on the blue living room sofa, studying a medical text-book. On my way to Ida's room, I peeked over her shoulder. Photographs of genitals blooming with sores decorated a page. I wondered what it was about Ida that had her mom convinced she was a lesbian. Probably that she looked so much like Kurt Cobain.

"Your mom is looking at pictures of herpes in the living room," I said.

"I know. She does that all day long. Last night, she started talking about a calcified fetus in the middle of dinner."

"What were you eating?"

"Stroganoff."

"Why was she talking about a calcified fetus?"

"She found one at work."

I imagined one in a desk drawer. I imagined one as a paperweight.

"Where was it?"

"In a woman. Wanna go to youth group with me?"

"OK."

"Wanna get McDonald's first?"

"OK."

We tore out of her bedroom and sped into town. We got a cheeseburger and fries, split them between us, and gobbled them up before parking under a magnolia tree. We headed to the buildings behind the church. Back there, the hallways felt schoolish. A brick propped open a door. We walked into youth group.

Three boys looked at us from their chairs. Their eyes moved up and down. I couldn't believe Ida didn't understand this. She went to youth group because she was in love with Jesus. Everyone else went for sex.

"Hello, ladies," said the boy in cutoff shorts. His head was shaved except for bangs. We slid into some folding chairs. I nodded at the other girls seated in the circle; three were Mexicans. One told me, "You look like an actress."

"Which one?" I asked.

"I don't know."

"What's she been in?"

"Movies."

"What kind?"

"Many."

Youth group got underway. Our leader, the apostolically named Steve, sat in a folding chair between the boy in cutoff shorts and the Mexican girl with the thicker sideburns. Steve was wearing flip-flops, cargo shorts, and a T-shirt with a surfboard on it. He was grotesquely good looking. I couldn't trust him.

Steve talked to us about Jesus. I watched the boys. They seemed interested in the Mexican girls, especially the big-titted one. One of the girls would leave to go to the bathroom, and then a boy would leave to go to the bathroom. A boy would come back. A girl would come back.

We played musical chairs to Christian rock, and then, after about an hour, Steve asked, "Who's signing up for the Mexico trip?"

Ida grabbed my arm. "You should come!" she insisted.

"Why?"

"Because you speak Spanish!"

Steve looked at me with interest. "You speak Spanish?" he asked.

I nodded. I looked at the Mexican girls. "You guys speak Spanish?" I asked.

They shook their heads. The one with a perm added, "Nope."

"You'd be playing a very important role if you came," Steve said in singsong.

"Please come!" blurted Ida.

I thought about the last time I'd gone to Mexico. It was three-ish years ago, when I was fifteen. I was supposed to go with Mom again this summer.

I asked, "How much does it cost?"

Steve said, "Nothing."

I grew extra suspicious.

"Where to?"

"Baja."

I narrowed my eyes and asked, "What's the point?"

Steve said, "We're going to spread the Gospel and build houses."

I stared at Ida. I stared at Steve. I waited a minute. I said, "I'll help build houses. But I'm not going to tell anyone about Jesus. They already know about Jesus. Mexico is filled with them."

// //

We were riding back to Ida's, the sun was setting behind us, and Ida was singing, "Our father, who art in heaven, hallowed be thy name!"

I joined, "Thy kingdom come, thy will be done, on earth as it is in heaven!"

We followed the tune that we sang the Our Father to at school Mass.

"Give us this day our daily bread and forgive us our trespasses, as we forgive those who trespass against us, and lead us not into temptation!"

Ida grabbed my hand, just like at Mass, and we belted, "For thine is the kingdom, the power, and the glory, forever and ever, amen!" Thrusting our hands to the roof, we screamed, "FOR THINE IS THE KINGDOM, THE POWER, AND THE GLORY, FOREVER AND EVER, AMEN!"

Our ears rang, our cheeks burned, and we laughed so hard the sound possessed the car like a demon. What we'd done wasn't for any father. It was to hear our voices in unison, to shout, to enjoy being animals together. We were animals deep in Eden. Animals that would never leave Eden. East, west, south, and north of a place that's no-man's-land.

Summer in Sumer

I spent the summer before I left for college peeing in a Mexican desert and trying not to strangle Christians.

Cyndi Lauper

"Girls Just Wanna Have Fun" was originally a kind of rapey song meant to be sung by a guy. Luckily, Cyndi Lauper saved it. She sang it and danced to it and used it to convert girls to feminism. Have you seen the song title parodied on tote bags that read, "Girls Just Wanna Have Fundamental Rights"? I have.

I wanted to have fun the summer before I left for college.

One of my favorite things is when people misspell *college*. I like it when kids go online to announce that they got into the collage of their dreams. It sounds so surreal. I imagine Salvador Dalí on the admissions board.

I got into the University of California, Berkeley. Because I'm Mexican. And pretentious.

I was thinking about college when Steve loaded a bunch of chaperones and teens, Ida and me included, into a station wagon and two Broncos. We caravanned to a Mexican village without plumbing. It was named La Huerta.

At night, since the outhouse was in use, I wandered into the desert to pee.

Squatting over the dirt and cloaked in darkness, I let my sweats puddle around my ankles. I tilted my pelvis back. I pulled my sweats' crotch forward to prevent it from getting a golden shower. I'd already killed my flashlight.

I considered scorpions. One could scuttle toward my wound and reach for it. She might trim my clit. I hadn't learned the term *female genital mutilation* yet, but I feared it. I would learn about female circumcision at school, in my women's studies classes. I think I minored in women's studies, but I'm not sure.

// //

The fact that I'm not totally positive about the minor reminds me that both of my grandmothers died of Alzheimer's.

In Spanish, *Alzheimer's* is *el Alzheimer's*.

Alzheimer's sucks in any language.

Aguita was the last word I heard my mom's mom say. It was the only word she could remember, I think. Adding *-ita* turns nouns diminutive. Abuela, abuelita. Agua, aguita. Abuelita was out of her mind, but she showed tenderness toward water.

During the last year of her life, a dentist pulled the teeth from my abuelita's mouth. We flew to Mexico to be with her toothlessness. Mom sat at her deathbed, dunking cotton balls into water. She traced her mom's lips with them. My abuelita stared at her ceiling fan. Its rotors spun. Its white string twitched. Death saturated the objects in the room. She presided. A framed portrait of La Virgen de Guadalupe observed the ordeal from above the headboard. Her Mona Lisa smile betrayed sadness.

// //

Death does have a gender. She likes to flirt.

// //

The summer I peed in a Mexican desert, I met some missionary expats.

They were Americans, a husband and wife, and both were beautiful. What is up with these modelesque missionaries? Can the ugly not serve as emissaries of the divine?

The missionaries were reformed party animals. They had a daughter, a little white girl who wore colorful dresses and barrettes in her hair. She sang to herself. Sometimes she played with Mexican girls. She bossed them around in Spanish. She told them, "Listen to me." What an imperialist.

When I wandered back from peeing in the desert, the missionaries' daughter was playing beneath pomegranate boughs. She suspended a doll over the dirt, making it shimmy. Its plastic hair shone. The girl's eyelashes looked plentiful in the campfire light.

I am a gringa, and since gringos are really good at exploiting Mexico as a liminal space, a shadow rose in me and eclipsed my morality. Images of violence toward the missionaries' daughter sped through my mind. I could smash her head with a rock, beat her with cacti, stab her with thorns, rip off her dress, destroy the world between her legs, and throw her in a stream glittering with fool's gold. The desert is a place where people go to be tempted, but I wasn't exactly tempted by these visions. The geography, however, did suit my spiritual revelation. The desert was behaving biblically. It was helping me to acknowledge that evil starts in the mind. Mine, Jeffrey Dahmer's, Moses's, John the Baptist's, anyone's.

Carl Jung said that it is not the light that enlightens us. The darkness does. Mexico is the place where this object lesson happened for Ambrose Bierce and me. Mexico didn't go as easy on Bierce.

OMG

I have something to confess.

I never finished reading *The Diary of Anne Frank.* I sometimes used to worry about whether or not I was going to burn in hell for finding her diary boring, but when I stopped believing in god, I stopped wondering about that.

Dorm

I bought a hefty plaster Buddha from a vendor in Tijuana. I made Steve rope it to the roof of the Bronco. He didn't want to because Buddha isn't very Christian, but whatever. The Buddha came to Berkeley with me. So did my copy of *The Collected Poems: Sylvia Plath*. And my favorite stuffed animal, a plush brontosaurus named Anton. He was named after the scientist, not the Satanist.

Mom and Ofelia stayed home while Dad and Herman drove me to college. We rode along the Pacific coast in a gold station wagon. Plum trees, eucalyptus trees, almond trees, and garlic fields flanked the road in increasingly northern counties. We lunched on hamburgers. We hardly spoke. I wondered if my terror was detectable. Going to college without Ida terrified me. She was going to the University of California at Santa Cruz. (That's where she got accidentally introduced to crack.)

Nobody warned us about move-in day pandemonium at the dorms. Families unloading sons and daughters jammed Berkeley's one-way streets. Cars filled with mostly white families parked wherever. Everybody except for Dad was breaking at least three traffic laws. Teenagers schlepped beanbags, bookshelves, and contraband pet rats up sidewalks. Moms lugged milk crates full of toiletries. Little sisters cried. Little brothers picked their noses. Dad verged on hyperventilation. He considers traffic crimes to be crimes against humanity.

"Look at all these assholes," he said. "Where am I supposed to park? They're parked in the street! You can't *do* that. You can't park in the *street!*"

"Just keep going," I urged. I clutched a copy of *The Bell Jar*. My fingers rubbed its velvety edges. "Just keep circling till something opens up."

I looked at Dad's face. Even his beard looked constipated. I felt his capacity for homicide. Its warmth emanated from his skin. He was capable of killing many of these people.

Dorms took up the block. Each unit rose like a mini-skyscraper. We executed a series of snail-paced right turns for half an hour till Dad craned his neck forward. His Adam's apple bulged. He stared. A metered parking spot had opened up.

A white girl hopped off the curb. She walked to the center of the open spot. Blond braids hung to her shoulders. She wore a T-shirt, khaki shorts, and Tevas. She had probably been a Girl Scout.

(Ida had been a Girl Scout. She had tried to get me to join, but I couldn't handle it. The pressure to sell cookies was too much.)

Dad switched on his blinker. He pushed the brake. He made eye contact with the white girl.

With haughtiness, she looked Dad in his half-white face and folded her arms across her chest. She yelled, "I'm saving this spot!" She was almost smiling. Her almost smile was what did it.

The white girl looked at something beyond us, at something we couldn't see. Maybe the white privilege fairy.

Dad rolled down his window. He craned his bald spot out. He shouted, "THERE'S NO SAVING!"

The white girl looked at me. She stiffened. She was steadfast in her colonization.

"That girl doesn't understand," muttered Dad. "There's no saving."

I looked at Dad's lap. His legs twitched. His foot moved toward the gas pedal.

"Dad!" I screamed. "Don't!"

He turned to me and shouted, "Honey, I HAVE TO." Looking at the white girl, he shouted, "THERE'S NO SAVING!"

The station wagon sped toward her. As we neared, her eyes grew to the size of hardboiled eggs. I could tell she played volleyball from how she leapt out of the parking spot. Onlookers stared at us like we were the assholes.

I shrank and prayed.

// //

The elevator was broken, so we carried my belongings up eight flights of stairs. No one else had arrived in the triple I'd been assigned. Bunk beds were stacked against one wall. A twin bed was shoved against the other wall, in between desks. Across from the desks, closets without doors. A third desk was parked beneath a mirror bolted to the wall.

Dad and Herman stacked my boxes and bags near the single twin.

"You're lucky," said Dad. "You don't have to share a bed."

I decided the head of my bed would be the end near the window.

Fall Semester 1995

ANTHRO 3AC
ART 8
EDUC 98
ENGLISH 45C

ID

In the cafeteria, I sat on a low stool in front of a gray backdrop.

A photographer said, "Smile."

My lips followed his instructions.

Magdaleno

Some people go to college to get a useful degree. They study hard for it. I've seen them. I've seen people carry laminated notes into the shower so they can multitask. I never showered with my homework, but I did study hard. I studied hard with the intent of becoming useless. I studied hard with the intent of becoming an artist, a revolutionary, or a saint.

Given what I knew about my family, and given my taste in books, I felt like I could really become one or all these things. I meant it when I said Marx made more sense to me than the Bible. My Mexican grandmother's hobbies were painting and praying. My Mexican grandfather had published several poems.

Some of my Mexican ancestors had rebelled against their government during the world's first communist uprising. People often believe the first communist uprising happened in Russia. It didn't. Mexicans tried turning red first.

One of these Mexicans was my great-great-grandfather, Magdaleno Escobar. He was a baker, a horse rancher, and a rebel. Federal troops captured him in the state of Colima and took him to the capital, also named Colima. In the plaza outside the municipal palace, a captor commanded, "Touch your nose to the wall!" My great-great-grandfather followed the instructions. Another Mexican ordered, "Fire!"

Years after his execution, his sister brought the revolutionary's daughter to the site of her father's last moment. The aunt told her, "Go ahead. Touch the wall." The girl traced bullet holes with her fingers. She wondered which one was made by the bullet that killed her father.

Magdaleno's wizened daughter gave Dad Magdaleno's story.

Dad gave the story to me.

I wonder how much truth could fill Magdaleno's bullet hole.

I hope none.

I hope the story is a lie or at least half a lie.

Mexicans are good at sitting on the truth. Octavio Paz knew this. He described our speech as "full of reticences, of metaphors and allusions, of unfinished phrases," our silence as "full of tints, folds, thunderheads, sudden rainbows, indecipherable threats."

I have a deep respect for big-time liars. They create religions. They create poems. They make art. Liars move us. Liars make us believe that Nietzsche was wrong. God can't be killed. Only hidden.

I really did believe that I had what it took to become what I wanted. People in my family made things. People in my family made things up. People in my family were shot in the back because of Karl Marx. People in my family had been poisoned, held for ransom, and tortured. I excelled at self-mortification. So did my sister. Suffering and not eating are the hallmarks of sanctity.

I didn't believe the anthropology, education, and English classes I'd signed up for were going to help me reach my creative or theological goals, but my art class would. It was titled Introduction to Visual Thinking.

A white man in black-rimmed glasses taught it. He lectured us in a small room down the hall from the Hearst Museum of Anthropology. Slides of Monets, Manets, and the professor's own work glowed on a large screen behind him. He leaned against the podium, elbows bearing the weight of his mediocrity, right hand gripping a clicker. The projector spat up its next image. More impressionism. Blah. Kind of boring.

The professor described how impressionism worked. He explained the art as if he had no soul, in an accent I couldn't place. I wanted him to devote a lecture to his accent and the reason for his sallow skin. Was he a Kennedy? He almost spoke like one but with a dash of palsy. Was he an alcoholic? His skin made me sad. He didn't seem tragic enough to be teaching art. His clothes seemed especially artless. He wore jeans and boring sweaters. I'd been expecting Jackson Pollock.

I love Pollock's last name. It's partly me.

Professor not-Pollock's lectures took place once a week. Attendance dwindled. By the second month of the semester, only freshmen were going. I, of course, was one of the faithful: in my seat by eight o'clock, spiral-bound notebook open and resting on the desk latched to my chair's arm. My pen flew, capturing every word this white man said about how my brain should interact with this planet's visual culture. I wrote about chromatic schemes and monocular cues. I rubbed the corn on my middle finger. I ran my fingers and the corn through my hair. It surprised me to find so little there. I kept forgetting I'd hacked it off at Supercuts in August. Short hair had seemed a humble choice. I'd become obsessed with humility since my desert epiphany. I wanted to be good. I didn't want to be a thinker of bad thoughts. I wanted to be a thinker of good thoughts.

Humility meant purity of word, thought, deed, and body.

I stuck my pen in my mouth. I sucked it. I daydreamed about Joan of Arc.

My childhood books about the lives of saints now sat on my dorm bookshelf. I wanted those legends near me. I thought of them as reference manuals. After reading the story of Joan of Arc for the first time, I'd wanted to grab the matches off the toilet tank and set myself on fire. I wanted to interrupt the lecture to tell Professor not-Pollock that was impressionism, that Joan of Arc was a better impressionist than Manet. She looked so like what she was—a tomboy saint—in Carl Th. Dreyer's silent film about her adventures, so heroic and fragile in the scene where a man's hand places a crown on her head. That scene proves that to be a saint, you must have a certain kind of face. It needs to have photogenic cheekbones. Mine weren't bad but they weren't impressionistic yet. I planned to pile less on my cafeteria tray to make them so. I vowed to eat fewer tater tots so my bones could catch the light and reflect it in holy tomboy ways.

// //

Introduction to Visual Thinking met in the art studio twice a week.

Most kids were taking it for the easy A; they weren't there to become artists. The ones who were there with that goal were clearly there with that goal. You could tell by looking at them. The artists owned paintbrushes but not hairbrushes. They wore jewelry heavier than everyone else's. They wore fashionably unfashionable footwear. A microbiology major who was taking the class for fun sat at my worktable. He was a ripped Asian who dressed normally, muscular with a very nice jawline. His name was Tim, and it surprised me that he talked to me so much. I was a troll. He was hot.

Staring at the back of an art girl's head, he sneered and shook his. He leaned toward me and hissed, "Art hair."

I knew what he was talking about. All this girl's aesthetic integrity was tangled in her hair. She out-arted all of us when she created a cardboard collage honoring her low self-esteem and crumpled during our critique of it. Her collage sat on an easel, we crowded around it and made our comments, and long tears slid down her long cheeks. She bolted out the studio door, fashionably unfashionable shoes clattering down the hall. Nice girls chased her. I didn't.

With admiration, or something like it, the grad student in charge of studio breathed, "She's so sensitive . . ."

Tim rolled his eyes. He muttered, "That bitch needs to brush her hair."

I suspected the grad student in charge of the art studio of lesbianism. She was a white woman and part ostrich. She wore her hair shaggy and feathered. She shared little about herself, so when someone asked her, "What kind of stuff do you like? What kind of art do you do?" we all leaned in.

"Fluxus," she answered.

A kid who'd seen her art whispered to me, "It's just a bunch of wood boxes."

Considering how dull she seemed, that made sense. Dry lips, dry hair, dry art.

One of our assignments was to make art in a non-art space. For this assignment, Tim wrapped a nearby spiral staircase in pink and purple string. It became something for students to trip on while doing psychedelics. We also had to appropriate non-art objects and make them art. A thick white girl who always wore overalls to studio reclaimed an abandoned recliner from the curb outside our dorm. She dragged it to the studio, painted it, duct-taped its holes, and glued a sketch of some guy's face to the crack between the seat and the back. She explained, "This work is about obsession." She pointed at the face. "I'm obsessed with him." She smiled. "He's beautiful. He's so beautiful."

He totally wasn't beautiful. The recliner was gross.

The grad student asked, "Does he know you made this?"

The artist giggled.

I thought mean things. I thought the word *tacky*.

Everything about the piece was tacky. It was offensively tacky. I felt sinful for thinking that. My stream of consciousness is very judgmental. My subconscious is and always will be a mean person.

For that same found-art assignment, an Asian girl added the word *greed* to a dollar bill as a critique of capitalism. Another Asian girl used oil pastels to recreate famed nursery rhyme scenarios. We peered at her sketch of Little Boy Blue. Tentacles sprouted from the ground as he napped against a mound of hay. The tentacles seemed ready to curl around him or tickle his bare feet.

One day, a racially ambiguous art girl with light-pink hair showed up at studio. I turned to Tim. "Her face is *soooooo pretty,*" I murmured.

"Whose?"

"Hers." My chin pointed at the pink-haired girl.

"Thunder thighs?"

I took note of her thighs, which I hadn't done before. They were thick. "Yes."

For every project our professor assigned, I used photographs. For my first assignment, I recycled a slab of pine from our studio's dumpster. I sanded away its roughness and bought acrylic paints from the art store across the street from the Hotel Durant. I painted the wood pale gray and, in what I thought looked like nineteenth-century cursive, listed the names of my family members in black. I added a white banner and wrote "we are seeds in a pomegranate somebody in hell clutches." I love melodrama. Near these words, I painted a crude yet baroque pomegranate with its insides exposed.

I glued pictures of Mom, Dad, Herman, Ofelia, and me inside the pomegranate's seeds. Five seeds. Saint Veronica.

During my critique, I propped this piece up on the chalkboard ledge. Artists and non-artists clustered around it. I explained, "It's a retablo. A Mexican ex-voto. I guess I gave it pagan undertones." My thumb pointed at the fruit. "Because of the pomegranate." I waited for everyone to talk shit.

They did.

For my next assignment, I cut ballerinas out of a Degas print I bought from a poster shop. I pasted their bodies to a pink velvet swatch that I glued to more recycled wood. I sat at my dorm desk, flipping through the small family photo album I had brought with me. I stared at pictures of Ofelia. She'd had anorexia. Or had she? Dr. Hamilton had insisted that her illness was impossible.

Regardless, she'd become a corn husk.

Aztecorexia.

I cut out pictures of Ofelia's gaunt face. My x-acto knife decapitated Degas's dancers' heads. I pasted Ofelia's where theirs had been.

When I presented this project, the graduate student shook her head. She said, "You can't use photographs for your next assignment. Try something else."

I hate being told I can't do things.

The graduate student wandered away from me. She strolled from table to table, handing out a sheet with a list of local art exhibits we could check out and critique. I skimmed it.

I paused on the first female name, Hannah Wilke. Her exhibit *Intra-Venus* was showing at San Francisco's Yerba Buena Center for the Arts. I didn't know who Wilke was or anything about her work except that it might have to do with being a woman. For that reason, I circled her name.

Her first name was a perfect palindrome: Hannah. hannaH.

Mine is an imperfect one: Myriam. mairyM.

Her last name ended in *K E.*

My middle name ends in *K A.*

I wanted this nonsense to mean something.

I wanted to cry eureka. Eureke.

// //

I could talk about the train ride to San Francisco and how grown up it made me feel to go to the city alone to see art.

I could talk about the time in junior high when Dad took us to San Francisco for vacation and I stared at everyone, even the pigeons, wondering, "Are *you* gay?"

I could talk about how the sunlight moves in San Francisco. San Francisco sunshine is a bisexual woman moving through the fog.

I could talk about ghosts in San Francisco.

Allen Ginsberg's ghost runs through North Beach. It streaks. Its ghostly penis flops. AIDS ghosts weep beside trashcans. Only certain people can see them.

None of these things matter, though. Not ghosts, Allen Ginsberg, or queer pigeons.

What matters is a woman making art out of everything she was born with.

I was standing in front of evidence of a woman doing exactly this.

Hannah Wilke was dead—the brochure in my hands told me so—but I was still watching her make art out of everything she was born with. The brochure explained that Wilke and her husband collaborated to make these photographs while lymphoma ruined her body. The brochure showed younger pictures of her with gum stuck to her face, chest, and back.

I put my face near her dying face. She looked pretty with lymphoma. I didn't feel bad thinking that. Her face reminded me of Mom's. It had good bone structure and a nose that was a natural work of art.

Maybe Wilke called this series *Intra-Venus* because she found Eros in dying. Eros is present in every image. In many, she seduces. She covers her face with her hands and swings her thinning hair. She does the things girls do that make boys think we like them. Wet hair hangs over her eyes and cheeks. She looks at the camera's lens through the thinning strands. This reminds you who's in charge. A palindrome.

There is Hannah (I feel I can call her by her first name because of what she's shown me) and she wears a puffy white cap. A bag is taped above her breast. Her black robe flops open. Underneath, tubes.

Hannah in house slippers.

Hannah in bed.

Hannah in a bathtub.

Hannah with a little bit of hair.

Hannah without any hair.

Hannah on the toilet.

Hannah wraps herself in a blue blanket and of course becomes the Virgin Mary, which is so much fun. Almost as fun as building a fort out of boxes and blankets. If you're a girl and a Catholic, you've done it. You've hoisted a blanket over your head and realized *this blanket makes me divine. Put me in a manger. Hand me my Messiah. Let's make one out of whatever is available. Women are resourceful. I will pretend that this bean burrito is the newly born Jesus. I will pretend that my fourteen-year-old cat is my donkey. I will pretend that this pillow stained by nosebleeds is my baby's daddy.*

Becoming the Virgin Mary is a good game to play when you're dying. It reminds you that you can cheat death and that you also can't.

Sunshine came into the gallery.

I ignored it.

Hannah Wilke was modeling how to be me for me. She was an artist, but she also had what it took to be a saint, at least in pictures. She taught me that most of being a saint is looking the part. Saints visually convince us of their power. They use props the right way. They especially use their eyes the right way. Blankets make them magic. Hair makes them magic. Less hair makes them even more magical. No hair makes them eternal. Their mortality looks timeless.

Saints are artists.

Other artworks hung in the gallery. I felt like maybe they were jealous of how reverentially I was treating *Intra-Venus,* so I walked over to them. They were pictures of beach houses. I couldn't give them what I was giving to Hannah. They didn't deserve it. I looked out the window and felt ill. I didn't have to love these other pictures. Maybe they were art, but they weren't a woman showing me how to become myself.

// //

I held my graded critique of *Intra-Venus.* Ten out of ten was written in green ink at the top. In the margin beside my second paragraph were the words, "Yes, I agree. She was BRAVE."

I watched the grad student's sweater sleeves jiggle while she passed back the other critiques. I said, "Excuse me?"

"Yes?" she answered.

"What do you find brave about Hannah Wilke's work?" I asked.

In a tone you use to explain the obvious, she answered, "Well, it's that . . . she was *so* beautiful."

I looked at the grad student like I needed more.

She added, "She was so beautiful, and she let us see that beauty destroyed."

I thought this was an unsatisfactory answer. Maybe the grad student's mom wasn't a beautiful woman whom she got to watch age. Every pretty woman who lives a long life gets to perform an art project called "watch my beauty disintegrate." It's not revolutionary. It just happens.

c c cummings

I shared my room with two girls of color. One of these girls was a rare thing for Berkeley: a Chicana. Her name was Ruth and she came from the outskirts of Fresno. She kept a framed photo of her dad shaking hands with Bobby Kennedy by the grim reaper bong on her desk. She had beauty like Hannah Wilke and Mom. She was so beautiful that she had a boyfriend. I knew when it was him on the phone because after answering, Ruth would say, "Yes, I accept," to the operator who'd asked her if she'd take a collect call from jail.

Ruth slept on the bottom bunk. She tacked a Metallica poster and a Metallica calendar up on her chunk of wall. She drew rosaries around her boyfriend's court dates. Inside the rosaries, she drew angels that looked more like bats.

Helen got the top bunk. Helen was Chinese. She taught me to say "shut up" in Chinese. She never studied for school. She sat at her desk studying hair manuals. One of her aunts sucked at English and was getting her cosmetology license. Helen was going to take the written part of the exam for her. I admired Helen for this.

I didn't, however, care for the way our dorm smelled. It smelled of dry humping and shrimp ramen.

I stayed in bed one morning with cramps. They were so bad they were giving me visions.

"Get up!" said Ruth. "Go to class."

"I can't," I groaned. "I'm birthing blood clots." My cramps martyred me. I deserved canonization.

I missed my English lecture. I was taking a class on modernism. I didn't know what modernism was; I just wanted to take an English class. So far, I'd sort of read *The Sound and the Fury* and *To the Lighthouse*. We were going to read *The Adventures of Huckleberry Finn* and *Heart of Darkness*.

While lecturing on *To the Lighthouse*, Dr. Brown drew an *H* on the blackboard. She explained, "This is how Virginia Woolf did it. Despite being stream of consciousness, there's a distinct structure to *To the Lighthouse*. Part one, 'The Window.'" Her fingers tapped the *H*'s left vertical bar. "Part two, 'Time Passes.'" Her fingers tapped the *H*'s connecting dash. "Part three, 'The Lighthouse.'" Her fingers tapped the *H*'s concluding column.

My classmates nodded. I drew an *H* in my notebook. I labeled its parts as Dr. Brown had done. I didn't care about form, content, structure, or *Mrs. Dalloway*. I wanted to hear about Virginia Woolf's suicide. I wanted to know how wet her clothes had gotten in the River Ouse. I wanted to know how many rocks it had taken to weigh her down. The best feminists are dead and wet.

The best feminists are martyrs.

Dr. Brown lectured to a mostly empty room. I always sat next to a black boy whose eyes invited me into his life. There was nothing malicious or misogynistic in them. They were filled with houndstooth scarves and homosexuality. He told me his name softly, "Nathan . . ."

Nathan liked David Lynch movies. He delivered gelato in the city. I could tell he'd had braces. His teeth were way too straight. He agreed with me that the class was stupid and that our professor kind of sucked.

Dr. Brown couldn't help sucking. Her voice cracked when she lectured, and her syllabus said that it was her first year being a professor. The first year doing anything new usually sucks, but Dr. Brown had the clothes part down—she dressed like an English professor. She wore earth tones and shirts that seemed like vests or vests that seemed like shirts.

She slurped black coffee while she lectured, and her hands shook so badly that the liquid sloshed over her paper cups' edges and spilled. Her silver watch caught the classroom light. When she waved her hands to make points, her armpits dazzled me. Matted tails spilled out of them. I'd never seen a woman with armpit hair like Dad's before. Mom always trimmed hers once it became stubble, and she'd bought me an electric razor and taught me to trim mine, too.

I modernized my armpits. I quit dragging a razor across them.

Our English reader held a few Xeroxed Harlem Renaissance poems, Woolf's "A Room of One's Own," some Salman Rushdie stuff, and a bunch of bullshit by Gertrude Stein that got on my nerves. I tried to read it, but it infuriated me. Alpha-Bits cereal. Its marshmallow letters float in milk and make no meaning. That was Gertrude Stein.

During her Stein lecture, Dr. Brown read an excerpt from *A Book Concluding With As a Wife Has a Cow: A Love Story*. "Nearly all of it to be as a wife has a cow, a love story . . ." she began, and as she got deeper and deeper into the piece, she read it with more and more Eros. It was gross. She made her voice cummier and cummier. Finally, once she was done, Dr. Brown said, "Stein was a lesbian. Her lover was Alice B. Toklas." She grinned. Her hand trembled. Her coffee cup quaked. Coffee spilled. She said, "This piece is about bringing a woman to *orgasm.*"

Nathan and I cringed. Dr. Brown hadn't committed completely to her cummy reading about the cows. To read a piece about lesbian e e cummings, you have to fully commit, but you could tell Dr. Brown was scared. The fright tarred her performance. It made it pathetic.

I looked at Nathan. We gave each other embarrassed smiles. Here was a straight lady (she talked about Mr. Brown sometimes) trying really hard to read a gay poem passionately. Nathan and I knew that we would have been better suited for reading this poem about gay cumming. Our eyes silently agreed on this. Our eyes shook hands on it.

Nearby, a thirty-something white lady student looked on, unaffected by Dr. Brown's reading. She crossed her legs and brushed her blond hair behind her ear.

// //

A pale student with dreads spent our entire time in English section diagramming how Joseph Campbell's hero's journey applies to *The Adventures of Huckleberry Finn.*

Overlapping circles covered the whiteboard.

It was so annoying.

I really didn't care.

The only thing I cared about in that book was racial dynamics.

Our TA was handing back our papers. She was a thick white girl with blond hair, a Norse name, and intense calves.

She set my essay facedown on my desk. I flipped it over. A scarlet *C* marked it.

The letter made me feel cold and wet.

I was not an artist, a revolutionary, a saint, or a genius.

I was a C student.

The TA set a paper on a desk by a tall window. Fir arms stretched past it. A black girl who often came to class in a leotard and sweats was seated at the desk. Her hair was pulled up in a Degas bun.

The TA pulled her leather satchel off her chair. She lifted it over her shoulder. She waddled out of the room with the dreadlocked student, whom everyone suspected she was fucking.

The ballerina flipped her paper over. Skinny tears spilled and wended down her cheeks.

"A C?" she moaned. "I've *never* gotten a C."

"I got a C, too," I said, hoping to console her.

Her tears continued. Her legs rubbed together. I felt sad for her. I tried sending good vibes to her bun.

I turned to Nathan. His scarf sailed over his shoulder. Tassels fell against his tweed jacket.

"What did you get?" I asked him.

"A C."

"Look!" I said to the ballerina. "Three of us got Cs!"

The ballerina said nothing. She was pretty when she cried. Bitch.

I shoved my C in my bag and walked into the hallway with Nathan. It smelled like wood and anxiety. I felt wooden and anxious. Like a termite.

// //

I was wearing my purple sweat suit and lying in bed. Ruth and Helen were away. I stared at the ceiling and pondered my C.

I C, therefore, I am.

Nicole

Of course an elderly white dude taught anthropology. Who better to explain all the cultures and peoples of the world than he who is in charge of them?

My anthro professor stood onstage in Wheeler Hall. His pastiness stood out against the blackness behind him. He wore his hair in a bowl cut. He wore cargo shorts, hiking boots, and a khaki vest bloated with pockets. He looked ready to dig or raid a tomb.

He lectured about a Kalahari Desert tribe.

Putting his withered mouth near his microphone, his tongue made a series of wet, sharp clicks. He clicked precisely and said, "Kung. An exclamation point in front of K-U-N-G is used to denote the click. The !Kung language contains many sounds not found in English."

The auditorium doors creaked open, but nobody paid much attention. Late students were probably trickling in.

"Yo!" someone shouted.

The professor stopped and the rest of us turned around. A lithe olive-skinned boy who lived on my floor stood in the doorway. His face appeared both frantic and elated. Excitement stiffened him. He seemed on fire to share.

He screamed, "THE JUICE IS LOOSE! THE JUICE IS LOOSE!"

Half the room gasped.

Some people laughed.

Some people applauded.

Some people groaned.

Some people booed.

I thought of white Broncos but not O. J. Not Nicole.

It was October 3, 1995.

Aesthetic Boners

You could do almost anything in and to our dorm. It didn't matter. Since they were going to remodel it, nobody gave a fuck. Kids punched holes in the walls, tore up the carpet, and peed in corners. Kids wheeled their office chairs into the hallways and raced. Nerd couples fucked in the showers. Blood smeared the toilet seats. Diarrhea splashed everywhere. Puke coated the sinks. Even though every gender used the coed bathrooms, no one got raped in them. They would have been a bad place for rape—too busy to get a decent sexual assault in.

Our room was crumbling. Ceiling tiles detached and fell on my body. They woke me up when I tried to nap. I breathed their asbestos. They flaked their cancer onto me.

Besides the ceiling tiles, I was kept up by coffee.

Coffee became my closest friend that semester. Coffee gave me everything I needed. Coffee made my heart beat faster and turned me into a speed reader. Coffee turned me into a sweaty introvert. One cup a day became six cups a day, either from the cafeteria or a café called Wall Berlin. Coffee stained Wall's floors. Students hung out at its wooden tables and benches, reading and talking theory. Artists hung out there not brushing their hair. I huddled in the corner studying anthro flashcards. *Homo habilis. Homo sapiens. Homo erectus. Australopithecus.* I prayed that I would become a saint who survived on kindness, crackers, and coffees. Saltines and americanos. Yin and yang. Gluten and adrenaline. I loved the way Berkeley coffee shops smelled. And the jazz they played. Listening to jazz made me feel smart for a Mexican, and the only thing that competes with the smell of raunchy, intellectual-bullshit coffee is the smell of stinky weed. Both smell bold. Both announce power. When you smell good weed or good coffee, you know you are smelling drugs. You know that you are smelling something that will do fun things to your brain chemistry.

Sometimes, just to change things up, I'd drink Mountain Dew. I was sipping the dregs from a can of it and staring at paint bottles left over from my pomegranate project. They sat on my desk near my word processor, which resembled a typewriter a computer had given birth to. Carrying it was a struggle. A tugboat could've used it as an anchor.

On the wall next to my bed I'd taped and pinned pictures of men and women I found beautiful: Sophia Loren, Isabella Rossellini, Damon Albarn. Italian women and English boys gave me boners. Not physical boners, really, but aesthetic ones.

I reached for the bottles of paint, uncapped them, and squirted a little bit of each color onto a dirty paper plate. I pulled a paintbrush from my desk drawer, crawled onto my bedspread, and fantasized that I was an artist. I dipped the paintbrush into maroon and dragged its tail along the wall. I dragged paint around the beautiful people's faces to frame them. I framed everybody, including Ida, with whom I'd posed in a photo booth for a strip of goofy pictures. That picture of us watched over my bed and so did one of Mom and me, her bathing me as a baby.

Underneath the pictures, I painted daisies in jars, premature green ones and feminine ones in reds and pinks. A crude flower garden proliferated and threatened to become a mural. I paused to assess and could see that Matisse had influenced it. I didn't even like Matisse, but you can hate your influences.

I painted a floating vase holding a single pink flower blooming at the end of a spaghetti stem. Below the vase, I painted the phrase, "A room is a room is a room . . ." The ellipsis indicated that rooms are always and forever being themselves. Roominating. I seemed to be operating under the influence of Gertrude Stein even though I hated her too. I'd read her long-ass poetryish thing titled *ROOMS.* In *ROOMS,* she rhymes the words *mister* and *sister.* She should've included *fist her.*

My window looked out onto roofs that shone after rain. I could see the smoky, foggy bay and Bay Bridge. I'd never lived up high. Having a bird's eye view tempted me to throw things out the window to see how fast they would fall.

I grabbed a bag of pork rinds sitting near Ruth's bong. I crept to the window, opened it, and stuck my head out. I reached into the bag, plucked an almost weightless piece of fried pigskin from it, and held it out. I watched as it sailed toward earth like an angel.

When pigs fly.

I tossed another and another and another.

I was watching one touch down on the sidewalk when a feminine hand appeared below. What the hell. I released another pork rind. It floated into the palm of the hand. Cradling the pork rind, the hand slipped back into the building. I felt satisfied that I'd fed somebody.

// //

We stood in the scary, tense semicircle students formed to criticize one another's art.

We were sharing our final projects, which were going to go in a student show. Since the grad student had put an embargo on my use of photographs, my medium of choice had become caloric and perishable. The grad student's eyes were fixed on it. She regarded it with approval. It stank on a stand that doubled as a painter's palette, welts of color giving it texture. The palette itself was modern art, a mini-Pollack, and my sandwich was plopped on top.

I made a sandwich.

Before class, I'd gone to a bakery and browsed loaves. I'd compared colors and shapes and settled on the most melodramatic. Wedging the challah into my armpit, I headed to the flower stand beside the donut shop. I purchased a bouquet of roses mixed with baby's breath. I stopped at the art supply store, picked up a tube of scarlet paint, and went to class. In my pocket, I carried a sliver of paper cut fortune-cookie style. The little slip bore my piece's title: "Dostoyevsky's Flowers, or Despair, Hope, and Redemption." The making of the sandwich was part of the piece. I'd watched people perform making sandwiches as art before. My high school friend Lindsay had worked at Subway and her nametag said, "Sandwich Artist." I'd watched her make roast beef and turkey clubs. I knew what I was doing.

I set the challah on a small paint-splattered table and knelt beside it. I tore it into halves and grabbed the bouquet. I unwrapped the flowers and shoved them between the pieces of bread so blooms stuck out at one end and stems at the other. I grabbed the paint bottle, shook it, uncapped it, and squirted red into the sandwich, across the flowers, and onto the palette. It was blood, fake blood, ketchup, a joke, whatever.

I pulled the title from my pocket, set it in front of the sandwich, and looked up at everybody.

"I like this," said the grad student. "I'm really into it. Food. Work that rots in multiple ways. Talk about it."

"I've been reading *Notes from Underground*," I said. "I can relate to the narrator's nervousness." Somebody snickered. Their snicker felt like a stab. I added, "I was also influenced by the installation pieces you showed us of those big hunks of cake suspended from the ceiling, gathering flies in that museum."

She nodded, pleased that I'd taken a cue from what she liked. She was really into those rotting cake sculptures.

"What about the rest of you?" the grad student asked. She looked at the bitch I was pretty sure was the snickerer.

A white girl with raw acne scars said, "It's beautiful and cathartic. I really like it."

The snickerer twisted her mouth smugly. The grad student asked her, "Jericho, what are your thoughts?"

Jericho drew out the word: "Weeeeeeeeeeeeeeeell. It doesn't really do much for me." She smiled. Silence.

I made eye contact with Tim. We shared the faintest smile. I imagined him force-feeding Jericho my sandwich and her shitting out the thorns.

// //

I got a C in English and a B in Introduction to Visual Thinking.

Like Raskolnikov, I suffered.

// //

I went home for winter break to get my first pap smear. I got it done at Ida's mom's office. She was between my legs, poking around inside me, and after taking her swab, she let my vagina shut its mouth. Tossing her speculum aside, she asked, "How's college goin', darlin'?"

I shut my legs and wept. I moaned something about Dostoyevsky and wanting to be a good person and not doing very well in my English class.

"Oh, sweetie," she said. "You know what college is?"

Through snot and spit, I gurgled, "What?"

Her blue eyes looked me in mine. She twanged, "It's the best of times, and it's the worst of times."

I recognized the quote. *A Tale of Two Cities.* I hated that book. All I remembered about it was decapitation and knitting.

Ida's mom got out her prescription pad and pen. She wrote something down, tore off a page, and handed it to me.

I didn't question why my neurosis had been recognized at the gynecologist, but I was glad someone had noticed that things were hard for me. Mom took me to the pharmacy, a pharmacist gave me a bottle of Zoloft, and I assumed a daily regimen of twenty-five milligrams washed down by six cups of coffee.

Spring Semester 1996

// //

I didn't know the new roommate had undiagnosed narcolepsy.

I just thought she was a bitch.

Helen had left and a white Mormon had taken her place.

She came from Phoenix, and she fell asleep while I talked to her. She fell asleep while reading Joyce Carol Oates (lots of us do). She fell asleep while peeing. She fell asleep in bed. She fell asleep on her cafeteria tray. Sleeping was like breathing for her.

"Hi, I'm Sydney," she said the day she and her magic underwear moved in.

Sydney, Ruth, and I took history 7B in Wheeler Hall. We sat together in the second row. One day Sydney split open a plain bagel. Her knife was spreading cream cheese across its pores as REM sleep struck. Her head fell back, landing on the padded seat. She continued to grasp her plastic knife in one hand and her bagel in the other. Eyeballs twitched under her pretty eyelids. Gooey snores escaped her mouth.

The professor, a white man with dinosaur teeth, gave her a scowl that was somehow tinged with awe. He was a good lecturer. He was a man, he was white, and he was *an excellent orator.* His expression said, "The audacity!"

A violent snore ripped out of Sydney. It knocked her out of her nap and her green-flecked eyes darted. Unsure what was going on, and seeming to remember that it was time for breakfast, she resumed spreading cream cheese across her bagel.

The professor carried on with his lecture on W. E. B. Du Bois's *The Souls of Black Folk.*

I glanced at Sydney. I glanced at the button on her lapel. The button said, "Verklempt."

Hart Crane

The history class taught by the old man with the dinosaur teeth became my favorite. Nobody molested me in that history class, and we read Ida B. Wells, Richard Wright, Betty Friedan, and Richard Rodriguez, though I wished we'd read Richard Ramirez. We read Richard Wright in comp lit, too, and there was a pompous, coked-out philosophy major in that class who was always inviting me to eat dinner at his dorm. I told him no. He sweat too much and his eyebrows were too sculpted.

One day he was standing outside our classroom door, shooting the shit with a curly-haired guy wearing gray sweats. The dude in sweats had an accent—he sounded Italian or something like that—and the coked-out kid introduced us. Soon after, the dude in sweats excused himself, announcing, "I've got Heidegger." He hurried away.

"Do you know who that is?" my classmate asked as we watched the gray sweats shrink.

"No," I said.

"That guy," he bragged, "is a prince."

The prince had been wearing velveteen house slippers. He seemed normal.

He wasn't my first. Two princes went to Berkeley. Sweatpants and a Norwegian. I shrugged. My classmate followed me into comp lit. He sat in front of me. I whipped out my notebook and got ready to take notes on a suicidal American poet who shouted, "Good-bye, everybody!" before he threw himself overboard, into the Gulf of Mexico, gaily losing himself at sea.

Babylon

Dad and Herman came and got me.

They took me home for the summer. Which was also the name of a white girl who lived down the hall. She had a piece of paper with her name written on it hanging from her door. I often fantasized about crossing out an *m* and making the sign Babylonian.

A Wrinkle in Time After Time

Consider this a prescient wrinkle in time.

Some of us use death to tell time.

Some of us use time to tell death.

The summer my abuelita died isn't really the summer she died.

The morning she died isn't really the morning she died.

The second she died isn't really the second she died.

The seconds she died aren't really the seconds she died.

She died all the time.

She died when she started forgetting things.

She died when her second child died during childbirth.

She died when my grandfather gave her gonorrhea.

She died when her third child was stillborn.

She died when her father left her on the steps of the stone orphanage.

Some of us use death to tell time.

Some of us use life to tell time.

Some of us use Jesus to tell time.

Anno Domini.

Ab aeterno.

Abhinc.

In media res.

Some of us use metronomes to tell time.

Some of us use baseball bats as metronomes.

Some of us use rape to tell time.

// //

When my abuelita was alive, she taught Mom to swaddle me.

When my abuelita was alive, she taught me to sit reasonably still.

She used horror, horsehair, and turpentine to do this.

I sat in a wooden chair in her moldering front hallway. She sat in a moldering chair near me, an easel propped near her knees. Knee-high stockings puddled around her ankles. One orthopedic shoe remained untied. "Don't move," she said. "Don't move."

She told me legends to keep me still while she dabbed a canvas with oil paints. She painted my portrait and told me stories. In one, revolutionaries rode up to a convent. They dismounted from their horses and lined up the nuns in the garden. Roses cowered as the men chose the prettiest women for violación. (Abuelita didn't explain violación, but its aftermath made my eyes bulge.) When they finished, the revolutionaries shot the nuns. The men didn't believe they were worthy of living to tell the tale of their violaciónes. The surviving nuns fled while the revolutionaries ransacked the convent. They discovered gold hidden in not-very-good hiding places.

Some of us use oil portraits to tell time.

Some of us use bullet holes to tell time.

Some of us use grandparents to tell time.

Some of us use the memory of our abuelita's casket, suspended by ropes and lowered into Guadalajara soil, to tell time.

Cyndi Lauper's saddest song is about time.

"Time After Time" masquerades as a love song. It suggests that you may get lost, but also that you will be found. You may fall, but you will be caught. Cliché is the drumbeat of "Time After Time." Romanticism is its heart. Cliché and romanticism form the backbone of modern memory.

Looking, wondering, circling, and falling.

"Time After Time" expresses the grief I felt staring down at my abuelita's stiffening corpse.

When we die, we fall.

Who catches us?

Cyndi Lauper?

Time after time is how a certain four-legged animal lurks. This beast has glassy eyes. Its fur is made of memories. It creeps up and pounces on you from behind. Humps your leg. Molests the clock inside you. Your second hand unwinds.

Hella Ukiyo-e

Going to college in the Bay Area made *hella* part of my vernacular, and since I'd done hella reading for school, I wanted to spend summer doing hella reading for pleasure.

And just because it was summer didn't mean I was giving up coffee. It was now time to enjoy coffee's full potential.

I was ready to hand my life over to caffeinated pleasures.

Since I'm susceptible to attractive book covers, I prowled thrift shop shelves and grabbed books with aesthetic appeal. Sexy sloppy seconds with smooth jackets and pages that had been fingered so hard they'd softened and swollen. I paid in coin for Kazuo Ishiguro's *An Artist of the Floating World* so I could double my pleasure: I could learn about Japanese art history while consuming a novel.

An Artist of the Floating World taught me more about ukiyo-e, an art form I'd developed some marginal childhood familiarity with. When I was eight, Dad had enrolled me in Japanese school. I was the only Molack there. I shared a high-ceilinged, chilly classroom with one class-mate, Yuka.

Yuka was Japanese American and not second generation. She was hella American, like third or fourth generation. Her inner elbow was crusted with eczema, and she would scratch it bloody then suck her fingers. She wore her hair in electric pigtails.

Dad knew her mom from work, so after regular school, on Japanese school days, Yuka's grandma cruised into our frantic school parking lot in her Cadillac. We rode across town to Yuka's, where we hung out in her bedroom. We stood next to a window framed with yellow ruffles. She played her Casio keyboard and we sang "You Are My Sunshine" to ourselves. We took breaks in her kitchen, where we stuffed ourselves with chocolate-covered Pocky and Hapi snacks, which are pretty much Japanese trail mix. Wasabi and seaweed flavored some of it. Yogurt never did, thank god. I hate it when yogurt sneaks into snacks. It's so unfair.

Once, in her bedroom, Yuka turned to me and told me to follow her. We went out, down her hall, and into the bathroom. Since she was creep-ing, I tiptoed. Yuka whispered, "Shut the door."

I obeyed as she knelt. Without making a sound, she pulled open the yellow cabinet door below the sink. Her scabby arms disappeared. She looked like a little plumber.

She emerged clutching a stack of glossy magazines. She set them down on the fuzzy yellow mat hugging the base of the toilet. Without any explanation, she opened one. I stared as she flipped through pages of ads that gave way to women who did not look like my mother.

My mother was the most beautiful woman I'd ever seen. That's not an exaggeration. My mother looked like Susan Lucci, the bitch from *All My Children,* but Mexican. Mom, however, didn't hop around doing the stuff the women in this magazine were doing. She didn't walk around wearing nothing but a robe and see-through heels while her breasts flopped out. Looking at these ladies was giving me warm-milk-before-bedtime feelings.

"Whose are these?" I whispered.

"Jerry's," Yuka answered. She called her dad *Jerry* for fun.

I grabbed a magazine and realized boobs were the best things ever. There were boobs and pussy on almost every page, and the boobs made me feel drunk or like I was on a cloud. They were so round. Gazing at that much pink stuff made me feel pink and grabby. I knew that somehow I wanted to connect my body to these bodies, and the faces mattered, especially the lips and the eyes. The expressions—lips parted, eyelids heavy—promised my desire was being returned. The faces communicated an invitation, and even though it was a performance, I was ready to ask these women to marry me.

I was eight, but I knew what I wanted.

I had access to cheap rings at the supermarket.

I wasn't sure what looking at the *Playboy*s, *Penthouse*s, and *Hustler*s did for Yuka. We didn't talk about what we were doing; we just stared together. The magazines might have given her that thrill you get when you look at something you're not supposed to look at. She might have been appreciating the beauty of the female form the way one does in a figure-drawing class. Or she might have been taking a bath in her own feelings like me. She stared at the brunette centerfold and scratched her eczema.

In Japanese class, we studied with our sensei, a painter/ceramist with a crispy black bob. Our sensei was born in Japan. She was married to an air force veteran, and she drilled us in both katakana and hiragana. She listened to us as we read aloud from Japanese primers. When we successfully completed a reading, she rewarded us by pushing a piece of stale cinnamon candy at us. Crinkling overtook the quiet as we unwrapped the cellophane. Our voices echoed as we said konnichiwa. O genki desu ka.

We were the only students at Japanese school. We counted ichi, ni (Yuka, me), san, shi, go, roku, shichi, hachi, ku, ju. We chanted ka ki ku ke ko. Sa shi su se so. N. Koi fish swam through our primers. They were aka to shiro. Blancos y rojos. Menstrual like Japan's flag.

Mom liked my sensei's art and bought a watercolor geisha from her. The artwork hung above my bed, a harbinger of my future ho-dom. Attending Japanese school taught me about femininity, nudity, and parting your lips a certain way: making sure people can see them forming vowels.

A, i, u, e.

O.

// //

Our neighborhood had mostly remained the same.

The obstetrician who'd cut me out of Mom still lived down the street. The family with the Mormon child who'd first exposed me to the sect's large underwear still lived there too, and so did the couple with the llamas that spat at you the way some men spit at whores. The Osmonds had relocated. Mr. Osmond was at Folsom, doing his best to avoid bending over. His wife and kids had moved into a condo that was less boy friendly. Shaquanda's mom was still hosting pro-life fundraisers at her house.

Around noon, I'd strap on sandals and go for walks along our neighborhood's sidewalkless streets. I sidestepped llama loogies while cradling biographies of famous women. I fell into their pages down by the abandoned barn. Feminism, the smell of hay, barbed wire. Sunshine that I didn't have to share with anyone. Weeds.

Having so much leisure time and freedom embarrassed me. I loved sitting in the countryside reading, but it wasn't constructive. It didn't seem fair. I decided to be a volunteer. I would donate my time to the library or some other quiet place.

I rode into town with Dad, and after leaving his building, I wandered across the train tracks toward a line of people waiting to be served free food at the Salvation Army. I left them behind and continued walking alongside the oaks shading the courthouse lawn. I left them behind too. Magnolia trees flirted with me near the public library's promenade.

I gazed at the bronze statue outside city hall. When I was five, Dad pointed to it and told me, "That statue is called *Mother and Child Miss the Bus*." While the statue might not actually be called that, it definitely conjures the mood.

I skirted the Methodist church, Chinese restaurant, and drugstore/ ice cream parlor.

A tiny art museum had opened next to the drugstore. Wisteria snaked up its tinted windows. I meandered into its pentagonal interior.

The art hanging on its tiny walls made me feel like my entrance was destiny.

Woodblocks depicting waves, mountains, cherry blossoms, sumo wrestlers, and pretty ladies abounded. They represented a microcosm of eighteenth-century Japan. I was reading about this kind of art. I was meant to volunteer *here*. With and for the art of the floating world.

Ukiyo-e.

I walked up to the liver-spotted, white-haired lady minding the front desk.

"Excuse me," I said. "I'm on summer break from college, and I'd like to volunteer here."

"All right," she creaked. "We're looking for docents." She smiled. I couldn't tell if her teeth were real. "You'll be the youngest."

"Good," I said. "I prefer the elderly."

The liver-spotted lady, Patricia, was right about my youth. My co-volunteers were five mature women, one for every weekday, and their companionship made me an interloper in a real-life version of *The Golden Girls*.

Staring at the empty gallery one afternoon, I sat beside a jellybean-shaped old lady, Muffins. Muffins checked me out and then fished a card out of her pocket and handed it to me. In a voice as alive as it was chubby, she said, "I'm a Poseidon Society representative." I wondered if this meant she oversaw gatherings for enthusiasts of maritime gods. I pictured green complexions, shells covering areolae, bubbles spitting from gills.

"Have you considered what you're going to have done with your remains?" asked Muffins. "It's never too early to start thinking about that." Looking at my neck, she asked, "How old are you, dear?"

"Nineteen."

Her second and third chins jiggled as she replied, "That's not too young."

I read Muffins's card. A trident pointed at her phone number in the corner.

"What *is* the Poseidon Society?" I asked.

"We're an organization that advocates cremation. It's the forward-thinking way of dealing with your remains. We also contract burials at sea." Muffins looked around the empty gallery in case of eavesdroppers. She lowered her voice. "There are certain places where we're not supposed to dispose. *I can make those disposals happen.*"

Interesting. Muffins was an ash pirate. I shoved her card into my smock pocket.

"I'll definitely start thinking about this," I said.

Muffins tugged at the tummy of her shirt. She looked pleased.

While sharing docent duties with the most flirtatious of the ladies, I discovered she lived in my neighborhood, in a house that looked like a Swiss chalet.

"Charming," she said to me, extending her hand. "As in, 'It's charming to meet you.' That's my name."

I wondered if Charming had suffered through a lot of Charmin jokes and figured she must have, so I didn't bring it up. It was the same thing with my old math teacher, Lipshitz. No one even bothered to mock him.

Aside from her name, Charming didn't really intrigue. But Patricia, the oldest old woman and the one I'd first asked about volunteering, did. I preferred hanging out with her. I got historically turned on as I listened to her share the lore of her life. She had that thing some elders develop where they compulsively narrate their youth while offering real talk a young person would censor. I thanked the goddess of old age for the days that this woman was my companion.

Once, we were talking about libraries and how I'd almost volunteered at one instead. Patricia said, "I read so much as a child."

"Me too!" I interrupted.

She continued, "I read every book they had at our library, and then I found books the librarian kept on a special shelf for books that I wasn't supposed to read, and you know what? I read those, too. That's how I learned about rape. A man would get a woman alone, trick her into a corner, and then . . . the chapter would end."

I told her, "I learned about it from my grandma! In Mexico, when we'd visit, she'd paint portraits of me, because she's a painter, and to get me to sit still, she'd tell me stories. She called rape *violación*. Like, in this one story she told me, some revolutionaries raped some nuns, and then they killed them, and while they were tearing the joint apart to look for gold, they found dead baby skeletons in the convent walls! Sluts!" I joked.

Instead of exclaiming, "Oh, dear! Your grandmother told you rape fairy tales?" Patricia said, "That's the word some of the books from the special shelf used, too. *Violate.* I've worked with women who've been abused and raped. I volunteer at a women's shelter, too, and some of the ladies," she folded her claws together and placed them in her lap, "I think they like it."

I mentally disagreed with her but said nothing. I respect my elders. Plus, I wanted to hear what bullshit she'd say next. (I sensed she had yet to be exposed to third-wave feminism.)

She went on, "We had one lady who came in and her husband had stuck his rifle inside of her and threatened her. She stayed with him. How could you stay after someone did that to you if you didn't like it?"

I thought I understood how a lady could loathe a situation like that but stay in it, but I felt ill equipped to explain this paradox. I was a C student.

// //

Nothing says you have a career in art, especially an unpaid one, like swaddling yourself in a shapeless black shroud. An art history teacher was coming to lecture us on the Japanese art exhibit he'd helped install, so that morning I'd slipped on a black blouse, black skirt, and black shoes. My hair color did not require alteration. Neither did the color of my soul.

I meant to bring the Ishiguro book to the art talk but forgot it on the kitchen counter with my purse. I walked empty handed across the train tracks, past the Salvation Army, the courthouse, the library, the church, the

Chinese restaurant, and the drugstore. I entered the art museum and sat among my fellow crones. We listened and nodded as the goateed art history teacher introduced himself and lectured us about the unbearable lightness of cherry blossoms. He droned on about Buddhist scripture, mulberry bark, urban pleasure districts, kabuki heartthrobs, and geishas, geishas, geishas.

I savored my smugness. I pursed my lips. I'd learned a lot of what he was telling us from my book.

The goateed art history teacher explained, "This genre of art is ukiyo-e. In English, that's—"

"Floating world," I interrupted.

The art history teacher's goatee gave a start. Have you ever noticed that sometimes it's not people's skin that reacts to the world, it's their facial hair? His goatee-mustache combo asked, "How did you know that?"

"I'm reading Kazuo Ishiguro's *An Artist of the Floating World*," I answered. "I also went to Japanese school." I smiled.

My smugness kicked up a Fuji-sized notch. I remembered the smell of the black ink our sensei made us dip our calligraphy brushes in. It had the faint stink of overripe mangos. I'd reveled in the fact that I could spell my first, middle, and last name in elegant letters that other kids couldn't read.

The art history teacher handed sheets of colored paper to us. I picked up an orange one, and he showed us how to fold our paper this way and that until we each had a paper crane. Again, something I'd done before. We pushed our flock to the sidelines, and the art history teacher gave us more paper and bossed us around, leading us in the creation of a basket.

Carrying a plastic bag of red-and-white peppermints, he walked from basket to basket. He held the bag over our receptacles and tipped it. Candies spilled inside. I felt like I was back in class with Yuka. I thought of titties.

At two o'clock, I carried the crane and basket I'd made to my cubbyhole. I set them inside and headed for the door. I growled "Domo arigato!" at the art history teacher.

Floating into the afternoon sun, I started my walk to Mom's work.

// //

I walked along the edge of the library parking lot, kicking magnolia pods out of my way. My black heels clicked. I turned the corner. Chemicals from the pool where I'd learned to swim freshened the air. I looked to my right. I sneered. The DMV. I'd successfully failed my driving test there three times. Historical fact: Cleopatra, the Virgin Mary, and Helen Keller never learned to drive, and they changed the world.

I crossed the street and sniffed at honeysuckle climbing the fence around the plant nursery. I headed past some weird brown building I assumed offered social services to women—I don't know why, but the building just gave off an abortion vibe. I crossed the railroad tracks cutting down the middle of the street. An old-timey Coca-Cola bottling plant loomed noirishly behind me.

The sky hung super clean, as if it had been Windexed. I thought maybe I had seen Elizabeth, the Lyon's waitress, back by the pool. I thought I'd spied her skinny body hurrying through the parking lot. Since she'd seemed in a hurry, I hadn't said hi. I'd chosen to ignore Elizabitch.

She was not a bad person. She was ditzy. People referred to her as Elizabitch because it was fun to say.

Elizabitch.

Elizabitch.

I stepped onto the curb in front of the rambling Spanish-style mansion that was my favorite house in the neighborhood. I meandered along the stucco fence rising beside the mansion's lawn. Here comes a classic moment.

// //

A possessive part of me wants to hoard this story. I want to chipmunk or squirrel away the memory of this event, place it in a tree trunk with the memories of all the other rapes, attempted rapes, and gropes, memories that will never be released or consumed. When a man asks, "What did he do to you?" he's asking to eat one of these traumatic acorns. Girls never ask for these seeds. They know what it's like to be degraded and fucked by this world, to be made a big-time bottom by life. They don't need the details of my particular shame to construct empathy.

Girls have always left my nuts, my tragic acorns, alone. Uneaten.

// //

I know I can be mean, but I also want to be likeable. I just don't want to be so likeable that anyone wants to rape me.

// //

Did you know PTSD is the only mental illness you can give someone? A person gave it to me. A man actually drove me crazy. He transmitted this condition. Like the man who gave my gay cousin HIV, or like my grandfather, who gave my grandmother the clap.

You can "get" schizophrenia or bipolar in the genetic sense. You might inherit genes that predispose you toward hearing voices or intense fluctuation of mood. In that sense, these conditions are "given" to you. But they aren't *given to you* in the same way watching your father cut off your mother's head on Christmas gives you PTSD.

// //

I want to be a likeable female narrator.

// //

But I also enjoy being mean.

// //

I always get crushes on people who are mean to me.

// //

I'm mean, but I'm not so mean that I've ever raped anybody. I've never grabbed a strange woman, pulled down her underpants, shoved my face into her pussy, and inhaled. That's a special kind of mean.

Omnipresence

My catechism teacher, a white nun with sky-blue eyes, taught me that god is omnipresent. He is a he and he is everywhere. He is in the sky. He is in the birds. He is in the grass. He is in you. Whether you like it or not, he is in you.

God is like rape.

Rape is everywhere too.

Rape is in the air.

Rape is in the sky.

Rape is in the Bible.

Rape happens at the neighbor's.

Rape happens at home.

Rape happens in the dugout.

Rape happens in the infield.

Rape happens in history.

Rape happens at bakeries.

I've watched children rape donuts with their fingers.

Rape gave birth to Western civilization and maybe your mom.

// //

Stranger rape makes me think of Camus.

// //

A stranger chose *me* to rape.

There was no nepotism involved.

Basically, I got raped for real. (I'm being cheeky here.)

Stranger rape is like the *Mona Lisa.*

It's exquisite, timeless, and archetypal.

It's classic. I can't help but think of it as the Coca-Cola of sex crimes.

// //

You never predict that rapists are lurking in the sun, sky, and trees. In other words, humans are as they seem. Seeming is real. After a stranger ambushes you and assails your private parts, everything becomes new. Everything is reborn. Everything takes on a new hue, the color of rape. You look at the world through rape-tinted glasses. You understand that you live in a world where getting classically raped is possible and that classical rapists lurk everywhere, even in impossible places. Like, is that a moth or is that a rapist? Is there a rapist hiding in that fresh-cut bouquet of sunflowers? Is that a rapist in your pocket or are you just happy to see me? It's a nerve-racking proposition. It's like being at the edge of your seat at a horror movie, but the horror movie is your life, and you're the girl who knows just how evil the ordinary guy is. This girl gets to live, but she understands that her job is to tell the story. Film theorists call this person "the final girl." Laurie Strode, the character played by Jamie Lee Curtis in *Halloween,* is a good example. Sophia is not. For every final girl, there is a cast of actors who must be sacrificed. It's all very Aztec.

Strawberry Picker

I'm unqualified to tell the story of Sophia Torres, but since she's dead, so is she.

A BOOK WITHIN A BOOK: THE SHORT, MEAN LIFE OF SOPHIA TORRES

PROLOGUE ,

The man who's about to sexually assault me murdered Sophia Torres. That's how I sort of know her.

I don't know her at all, really. I've never seen her, never touched her, but the man who touched me touched her too. Sometimes I feel like I know her better than I know most living people. We share this thing. A man, a Mexican. All three of us, the trinity of us, are Mexican. She and I share a fear of him. We share what it's like to have him touching us and watching us. Breathing on our faces. We both understood that he wanted us dead. She wound up dead. I mostly didn't.

Besides having survived, there are other ways I differ from Sophia. Although I'm Mexican, I grew up in a nice house with books, cable TV, and a white cleaning woman. I grew up with middle-class pleasure and privilege. Sophia didn't. She came to the United States from Mexico, picked strawberries for white people, and had a boyfriend who got murdered. She got raped, beaten to death, and left in a park. I can almost hear the Statue of Liberty whispering, "I'm sorry . . ."

It's not fair that I've had so much privilege. And by privilege I mean life.

The privilege of surviving doesn't feel good. It makes me feel guilty. It makes me not want to enjoy strawberries.

Parts of Sophia must've looked like strawberry compote once he was done with her. Sauce in the moonlight.

THE ONLY CHAPTER: MOST OF IT HAS ALREADY BEEN GIVEN AWAY BY THE PROLOGUE

There's hardly anything to say about Sophia. I learned about her by watching TV. A local news anchor referred to her as a transient who'd been bludgeoned to death in Oakley Park. The rest of what I know I've gathered from newspapers and court documents. Articles with headlines like "Battered Body Found at School" gave me bits and pieces. These headlines shared space with others that read "Heavy Rains Leave State Pretty Soggy" and "Two-Snouted Pig: Remains of Ditto Will Help Science." Her murderer's appeals are the documents that hold the most information about her life. The words "Appellant's Opening Brief" are centered in the middle of one page. The bottom of this page is stamped crookedly: "Death Penalty." The brief has a section devoted to Sophia's life. It says that Sophia was born in Mexico in 1961 and came to Arizona. She had a boyfriend, but somebody shot him or stabbed him or something. This made her depressed. She wandered from Arizona to California. She wandered around town. She spent her time quietly eating lunch at the Santa Maria Salvation Army. She kept to herself. She picked strawberries. People accused her of being withdrawn. One night, under the full moon, a guy, a very normal-looking guy, struck her with something over and over till he destroyed her face. He put himself in her vagina, too, and got cum on her dress. The police found her stuff strewn around the park. This trail of personal belongings means that he terrorized her, chasing her and chasing her before he turned her into nothing.

Exquisite Corpse

I hate found poems. Found poems are so tacky. That said, I used court documents to make a found poem for Sophia. I think it's a suitable tribute. Police found her in a park. They collected bits and pieces. All I know about her are bits and pieces. Rape cuts everything into bits and pieces.

                          5' 2"
                      drew a sample
                    of fluid from each of
                   the victim's two eyes she
                    would watch television
                         stare a lot
                             as
                             if
                           really
Señora,   thinking about something born in Mexico San Luis Sonora   *Señora*
skull   135 pounds came to the United States 23 years old speak   *alien*
card   English always a long blue jacket carried a black   *rigor*
mortis   purse creative very neat and clean person   *arm*
was   in the street usually walking always alone   *not*
stiff   worked temporarily at a bar Los Tres   *lift-*
ed   Amigos quiet not appear to   *the*
body   consume alcohol or drugs   *pla-*
ced   too inhibited   *it*
on   independent   *a*
she-   hard-working   *et*
we-   very meek   *st*
ea-   boyfriend   *st*
b-   killed   *-r*
-o   in   *-k*
-e   Arizona months two weeks   *-n*
-o   when victim returned acted depressed   *-f*
-f   S   very different 1994 quiet timid shy   T   *-f*
-i   R   introvert sign-in lists for November   A   *-n*
-g   W   14 and 15 ate lunch at the Salvation   B   *-e*
-r   E   Army take her plate of food   R   *-n*
-a   R   sit by herself Santa Maria   R   *-i*
          Y   worked in the strawberry   F
          I   fields sold pans   E
          L   and Mary Kay   D
          S   cosmetics   F
          O   R
          E   V
          E   R
          S   T
          R   A
                                                       W

B
          E   R
                         R   Y
          S
       HORT   CAKE
            SHORT   CAKE
                                                   CAK   E

                 E

Siluetas

I really feel Ana Mendieta's artwork, especially her siluetas.

I'll repeat myself and say that Mendieta traveled this planet's dirt, nestling herself into it and photographing traces of her presence. In some photographs, her trace appears as an unadorned impression. In other photographs, flowers fill the emptiness.

Every year, on the anniversary of Sophia's death, I take her flowers. I rest them on the dirt near home plate. They're my attempt at a tribute, an acknowledgement, but when I look at Mendieta's siluetas, I wonder if she was psychic. I wonder if she made these for Sophia.

// //

When you have PTSD, things repeat themselves over and over and over.

Guilt is a ghost.

Guilt is a ghost.

Guilt is a ghost.

// //

Have I told you about Ana Mendieta?

// //

It seems a long, long time ago that this story
first took place; of two young ambitious lovers
who wished to see an amazing grace. It's often
said you can't resist a calling within the heart;
with [me] and [you] this is how we start.
A gentleman, a lonely man, a gangster as well;
upon first sight of [you], [I] knew [I]
fell. [I] passed her by, [I] caught her eye, her
heart had skipped a beat; yes, [I] would be the
lucky man to *knock her off her feet.* The

aspect of this love unique is hard to
comprehend. Impossible, most baffling, when
analyzed from end to end; love between a boy
and girl, two hearts that beat as one; they hunger
for each other's *touch* with *passion on the run.*
They love to live and live to love together as
friends; yes, *this is the truth and story of*
[you] and [me] from beginning to end.

// //

That poem belongs to a legal document. It appears in his death-penalty
appeal. Guess who he wrote it for.
　　His girlfriend.
　　This poem proves he's a romantic.
　　Wordsworth.

I Wandered Lonely as a Dissociated Cloud

So I was walking, minding my own business, when hands circled my ribcage and slid down to my waist. They gripped me.

"It's Elizabitch!" I thought. "She's come to surprise me!"

My thoughts happen in lasagnas, in layers of meats, noodles, and cheeses, and the thought under the Elizabitch one was very different. It contradicted the one that believed a girl was touching me. This layer of awareness knew that the person touching me was not girl.

It was man.

But underneath was another layer. It breathed, "Men don't do things like that. They don't do things like that to *you*."

I chose to believe in Elizabitch.

I said her actual name aloud.

There was no Elizabethan response.

My thoughts shifted, on the verge of doing something psychologically seismic. The arms holding me felt very strong. The hands gripping my abdomen were large. A palm pressed into my navel.

Whispering her name, I turned around.

The man standing behind me looked so average it horrified me.

His grin horrified me the most.

He was enjoying our closeness, relishing it, pressing himself to my backside, holding me captive. We were close enough to kiss. I saw the stubble in his pores. His smile overwhelmed me and the rest of his face vanished. Only his mouth remained. A smile held me captive.

I broke up with my body.

Birds watched my assault.

I joined them.

I observed.

I saw myself in the clutches of a stranger waiting to do something to me.

I was a bird, though I was also myself. The smile looked into my eyes. I couldn't make sense of it. An animal part of me understood its intentions, but the intellectual part of me, the part that likes books and fantasizes about visiting the Louvre, didn't. It ignored the animal. My rational mind wanted to believe that a smile is a smile is a smile is a smile.

The man shifted his hold. His arm tightened around my waist the way safety bars hold riders in place on roller coasters. The smile descended. It lowered until it was crouched behind me, kneeling. Was he going to pray? Was he ready to receive Communion? Was he going to be knighted?

He was wearing mesh shorts, a T-shirt, and athletic shoes. He seemed about my age.

His face pressed against my ass.

He lifted my skirt. Fingers were in me, his breath and his mouth were on me, and the rest of the details belong to me.

The only other detail I'll give is one that seared me with humiliation.

"Oh my god," I thought, horrified. "I'm wearing my period underwear."

Girls know what I'm talking about.

// //

There was a point at which I heard my voice.

"What are you doing?" it screamed.

He continued doing what he was doing.

"WHAT ARE YOU DOING?" my voice roared.

He let me go and sprinted toward the corner. He looked over his shoulder and smiled.

Like a mouse chasing a lion, I ran after him.

He turned a corner, then another, and sprinted down an alley. I paused at the alley's mouth.

I quit there. My instincts told me to stop. They told me that he wasn't done and that if I followed him, he might finish.

// //

I went back to the corner where he'd crept behind me.

Where had he gone?

Tears welled. I was determined not to let them fall.

I didn't want him to see me cry. I didn't want to give him another chance to relish my fear.

I could feel him. Watching.

My heels clicked. The only sound in the galaxy. My skin prickled. It felt like he was in everything.

He wasn't finished.

Things like that are never finished.

Men like that are never finished.

I used to love the houses in that neighborhood. Covered in jasmine and ivy. They were so beautiful. *The Secret Garden.* My secret garden. After he touched me, it seemed like every fragrant bush might be holding him. He might be hiding inside that bougainvillea. He might be disguised as a butterfly or a hummingbird. Why hadn't I noticed him before?

Because he was everywhere.

I walked past the gray house where I was babysat in elementary school.

My feet crossed the street. Loaves hung in place of my arms. These limbs felt less mine than the rest of me, which also felt less mine. I was losing myself in degrees.

These sidewalks were so familiar. It amplified my horror that I'd spent much of my childhood walking them.

I walked to the spot where a cyclist once nearly ran Ida and me off the path. Ida shook her fist at him and yelled, "Asshole!" and he dipped into the street, U-turned, and pedaled back. "He won't," I thought, but he aimed his bike right at us. I leapt out of his way. Ida pressed her feet to the sidewalk, a righteous blonde. Tires sped toward her and cut right across her sneakers. The pressure caused her toes to bulge.

As the bike's rear wheel released Ida's foot, she flew backwards onto the lawn. She howled. I tried to hold it in but I laughed. Ida was crazy.

That was the meanest thing I'd known to happen on these sidewalks till today.

// //

Since I wasn't me, I don't know who was walking.

I don't know who was walking along those pretty houses, down the streets lined with pepper trees.

Mom had been a chemist in Mexico, like Marie Curie, but she was no such thing here. Here, she was a phlebotomist and then a third-grade teacher. She taught third grade at the elementary school I had gone to with Ida.

I walked past a lawn dotted with ornamental plum trees, past the school's library, along a cement walkway to Mom's classroom door. I opened it, stepped inside, and couldn't hold it in anymore.

I bellowed new words in a new language.

From their desks, Mom's third graders stared. Their mouths fell open. Mom's mouth fell open. The color left her face. Just like when I told her I was gay.

"Que pasó?" she insisted.

I might've said, "Somebody hurt me. A man."

Mom left the blackboard and ran to me. She reached for the phone bolted to the wall near my elbow. Grabbing its receiver, she dialed zero. In her strong Mexican accent, she said, "Send the preenceepal now. NOW."

Seconds later, we saw the principal coming down the walkway.

Mom took me by the arm and tugged me outside. She and the principal exchanged words, and I followed the principal back up the walkway, past the library and the plum trees, and into the main office.

The school secretaries turned as we entered. They looked at me. They had the same looks on their faces the principal had upon first seeing me. It was one I'd never seen before but recognized immediately. It was the oh-god-she's-been-raped look. It was rotten to receive that look. I didn't ever want to be looked at that way again.

The principal led me into the nurse's office. I sat near the sink. On the counter there were glass jars filled with cotton balls, cotton swabs, and tongue depressors. By the window stood a bed, and beside it, a scale. I'd been weighed on that scale once. I'd been checked for scoliosis in this office and had curled in that bed, wracked with nausea that made me retch and whine.

An eye chart hung behind the nurse. She roosted in a wooden chair beside the bed. She was a blond woman with huge tits and no waist. Her hair was platinum and fine. Her name alliterated.

"What happened?" she asked. She squinted at me through her glasses. She folded her arms and crossed her legs. She was closing herself off. The principal was gone.

Her question triggered a fresh round of hysterics. I wailed through my tears. "Iwaswalkinghereandamangrabbedmeandhewouldn'tletmego andhebentmeoverand—"

"STOP CRYING!" yelled the nurse.

Her command shocked me silent.

"You're going to have to get over this," she said. "These kinds of things happen. You're going to have to get over this. Do you hear me?" Her forehead tensed. Her skin grew stern.

I became perfectly quiet. The nurse observed me. Her expression remained firm. Sensation left me. Numbness replaced the volcano I'd been seconds before.

Somebody knocked at the door.

The nurse opened it.

A Latino man stood waiting. He wore a gray suit. Last time I'd seen such a man, he'd pulled down my underwear and done things to me.

"Yes . . . ?" she said to him.

"Hello," he said to *me*. "I'm detective Steve Lopez." He gave the nurse a good-bye glance. She waddled out.

He pulled the door behind him but left it slightly ajar. He leaned against the counter and slid a notepad and pen out of his breast pocket. He flipped the pages till he arrived at a fresh one. Pen poised, he asked me my name. I told him. He said, "I'm sorry, but I'm going to need you to tell me what happened so I can help you. Can you tell me what happened?"

I nodded and began to recite. I left out the part about calling him Elizabitch.

As I spoke, the detective wrote down what I said but never looked at me.

His skin, however, betrayed his humanity. It twitched at details of my peculiar, particular humiliation. Feeling breath on my pubic hair. The word *panty liner*.

In a distant part of me still capable of feeling, I catalogued and appreciated his winces.

"We're going to go back to the area where this happened to see if we can spot him, OK?"

I nodded and followed him out of the nurse's office. Reentering the main office, I saw Dad standing beside a spider plant in a macramé sling. Who had called Dad? What had they said?

The three of us headed out into the parking lot, to Detective Lopez's sedan, and I got into the backseat. Detective Lopez drove us to where I had been ambushed. I pointed to the corner where it happened. He parked and I walked him to the spot. I stood in it. I said, "It happened here." I walked to the alley and pointed. "That's where he went."

Detective Lopez said, "He's not here. We'll keep looking."

The three of us piled back into his sedan and cruised the perimeters of the rail yard, the pool, the library, and the DMV. The smile didn't stare back at me from any of those places. The smile had retreated into the small town ether, taking stolen sights, smells, and tastes with it.

// //

On our way home, Dad and I shared a big jar of tense silence. I broke it.

"The detective is Mexican," I said.

"I remember him from when he was little," said Dad.

Remember, Dad had first come to Santa Maria to teach elementary school. He taught hundreds of kids before becoming an administrator. We couldn't go anywhere in town without him being recognized by a former student.

"Was he your student?" I asked.

Dad nodded. "Fifth grade."

"Do you think he remembered you?"

"I know he did."

"How?"

"He said, 'Hello, Mr. Gurba.' You didn't hear him?"

I stared at Dad. It horrified and comforted me that one of his former fifth graders knew what a stranger had forced upon my crotch. I looked away, toward the broccoli fields. I can't remember anything about this day after that moment.

Jeans

A few days before I headed back to Berkeley, Detective Lopez called.

I felt like I was on an episode of *Law and Order* when he said, "I'd like you to come down to the station to look at some pictures."

Dad went with me. We walked together through the station's tall castle doors, and Dad told the receptionist, "My daughter is here to see Detective Lopez."

The receptionist paged him, and he led us to a high-tech room with monitors. He escorted me to one.

"This is a database. It contains photographs of known offenders. Please look at them carefully and take your time. Let me know if you see him."

Standing at a screen mounted at breast level, I scrolled through mug shots. They floated against a pixelated blue background. Most of the faces seemed Latino. A few wore lipstick, eyeliner, and blush. One wore a wig cap. I thought about how some of these "offenders" probably should have been recategorized as female, but I didn't feel like getting into a conversation about gender theory with the detective.

I paused at a mug shot of a tall guy who used to hang out with us at high school parties. He bought my friends and me beer. I clicked and scrolled till Mr. Osmond appeared.

"Not his type," I thought.

Perpetrator after perpetrator stared at me, unblinking, but none of them had smelled or touched me.

"He's not here," I said to the detective. I felt disappointed but also relieved I hadn't had to see his face again.

"Thank you," he said. "I'll be in touch. If you need anything, call me. You have my card."

The words felt so scripted. Stiff and preordained.

// //

Dad screamed, "Go change, now! Those jeans are ripped! Do you know what that makes you look like?"

He was implying that torn denim sent an invitation: this girl has holes . . . explore them.

I defended my fashion choice by shouting a slogan I'd heard a hysterical feminist shout on a TV talk show: "WHAT A WOMAN WEARS HAS NOTHING TO DO WITH WHETHER OR NOT SHE GETS RAPED!"

My throat did strange things to the word *raped*.

I silently doubted my defense. Had I not been wearing a skirt, it wouldn't have been so easy for that smile to go where it didn't belong.

Skirting the issue: I sometimes fantasize about meeting the inventor of the skirt. I fantasize about talking to him (because you know it was a him) and asking, "Why?"

My theory is that skirts exist to create a funnel to a tunnel. Good girls use their knees as tollbooths.

// //

I wasn't an art volunteer anymore.

Nobody wanted me walking around town by myself, so I spent my days with Mom: helping in her classroom, running errands with her on the way home. Since I loathed food shopping, I usually read magazines in the hair care aisle when we went to the market. One afternoon I felt too jumpy to be alone, so I walked down the bread aisle with Mom.

She pushed our cart. Michael Bolton flowed out of speakers. Somehow, I became queasy while simultaneously leaving my body.

He was approaching me.

Beside the whole grain loaves, he paused.

His hand reached for hot dog buns. It squeezed.

I came back to my body almost as immediately as I'd left it when I realized the shopper was not *him*. His was not the smile I still felt between my legs, like the worst kind of dingle berry. This shopper was some random homey, but for a sesame seed of a second, my mind transposed *that* face over this homeboy's face. It blended them into one composite. The post-traumatic mind has an advanced set of art skills.

The shopper stared back at me, reflecting my staring problem. I realized that he *could* be here shopping, maybe even with *his* mom.

Oh my god. He had a mom. Maybe they were here together, checking the expiration dates on egg cartons. Arguing about whether to buy corn or flour tortillas. Maybe she told him, "Bring me a bottle of Vicks VapoRub." Mexicans use VapoRub to treat everything. Smallpox. Emphysema. Miscegenation.

In terror, I moved closer to Mom.

"What's going on?" she asked.

"Just keep shopping," I insisted.

Each aisle brought the possibility of seeing him. I imagined him lurking, stocking up on Tang or Otter Pops. I saw flashes of him in nearly every man. The curve of a shaved head was him. A sharp grin was him. A bright white T-shirt was him. Tightly laced Nikes were him. Five o'clock shadow was him. Post-traumatic omnipresence. I wanted to burrow between Mom's legs and hide where I'd come from.

We made it to the checkout line. Fresh tabloids tempted me from their racks. Impulse buys in glossy wrappers gleamed. Bags of M&Ms. Disposable cameras. Nail clippers to attach to your keychain so you could groom yourself in the driver's seat.

I reached for *People* magazine and saw him. He was standing behind us, manning a shopping cart. Supermarket lighting cast an aura above his shaved head. Behind him, bakery display cases showcased yet-to-be personalized sheet cakes.

As quickly as the shopper had become him, he unbecame him. He settled back into his own features. My eyes adjusted to the similarities. The shopper's black eyes hadn't seen that part of me. Those nostrils weren't the ones that had smelled me.

I looked at the shopper's little girl. She stood beside him in a balloon-print dress. I hoped her dad was not the kind of man who did things like those that had recently hurt me.

Fall Semester 1996

ANTHRO I

HISTORY 8A

PHILOS 8

WOMENST IO

// //

I was living in a new dorm, the one closest to campus. This girl, Yenifer, was lumbering up our hall, wringing her hands. Grease and tears slicked her moon face.

"Yenifer!" I cried. My phone sat in my lap like a cat. My back was pressed to the fire-escape door. "Why are you crying?"

Yenifer replied, "Be! Cuz! Tu! Pac! Died!"

"Oh my god," I thought. "This bitch."

"What's happening?" Ida asked through the receiver.

"Apparently, Tupac got . . ." I made gunshot sounds.

Yenifer lived at the opposite end of the all-girls floor. It'd been a few weeks since what'd happened on the sidewalk on the way to Mom's, and I kept telling myself it was no big deal, it was nothing.

I was living in another triple. This semester's roommates, Carmen and Shakira, shared the bunk beds. Both were Latina. This made me trust them. Carmen, who slept on the bottom bed, aspired to be a surgeon. Shakira, who slept on the top and did crew, aspired to be surgically attached to Carmen. They were kind of lezzy except for the fact that they exclusively dated Latin and Persian dudes.

During the week we used to get to know one another, Carmen, Shakira, and I sat on our thin carpet, sharing bags of meat and talking. Carmen and Shakira told me they'd spent most of their summer partying at San Francisco clubs and being hit on by hairy men who glanced at their watches when asked, "How long have you been in America?"

Carmen asked me, "How about you? What did you do over the summer?"

I said, "I volunteered as a docent at a museum and got sexually assaulted." I described some of my rape, contextualizing it as NBD, and when I finished, Carmen was laughing.

"I can't believe you chased him!" she squealed. "You are *such* a Latina!" She snorted and squeezed my arm. Her nipples bounced. (She was topless. She was always topless. She was unashamed of her tiny tits.)

Carmen sounded proud of my Latinaness. This made me proud of my Latinaness. Of our Latinaness. She passed me a small bag filled with llama jerky.

Her parents came from Chile.

Shakira's dad came from Ecuador. Her mom didn't have to come. She was American.

One Saturday, a Persian admirer of Shakira's stood by my closet door. He stared at a picture of Mom I'd taped to it.

"Damn," he said. "Who's that? She's hot."

"I came out of her," I said.

Discomfort tightened his face. This made me smile.

That semester, I became fixated on two things: homework and exercise. I aspired to a 4.00 and a hard body. In the cafeteria, I placed only fruits, vegetables, and peanut butter on my tray. On Telegraph Avenue, I marched into a cheap salon and asked the hairdresser, "Have you seen *G.I. Jane?*" She Joan of Arcly chopped the hair I'd been growing. Acne cobbled my cheekbones. I wore sweats in public. I was becoming a prophylactic.

When I wasn't studying, exercising, or attempting to make myself neuter, I allowed our floor's mini-dramas to entertain me. An Indian neighbor to our left was involved in one. She was leading a campaign to get Apu, the Kwik-E-Mart owner from *The Simpsons,* off the air.

"Racism!" she raged. "Apu is a racist stereotype! He is a caricature and detrimental to Indians!"

I nodded while a bitchy voice in my head snapped, "Quit trying to bleach your beard. It's not helping." Of course I didn't express this thought to the activist. Such thoughts aren't meant to be said aloud, but I suspect everyone has them. Even saints.

Some female saints grow beards.

As an ethnic rite of passage, Mom taught me to bleach my moustache. Up till this semester, its yellow glow would've matched the Indian girl's muttonchops. Now I allowed its darkness to ride my upper lip.

Yenifer, the hysterical Tupac mourner, lived at the end of the hall. She intrigued me. She claimed to have been a renowned vocalist back in East Los (that's what she called East Los Angeles), and she was dieting to get back into a pair of skinny jeans she'd worn in high school. She pinned these pants to the wall beside some Christian arts and crafts for thinspiration. Their tag read "size two," and Yenifer's thyroid was not going to let her turn back the clock—not without a shero's journey.

Yenifer and I stood by her dresser. She pointed at the pants. In her deep, serious, Chicana accent, she promised, "I'm gonna be like that again. Te lo juro."

Yenifer spent a lot of time scaring girls out of our floor's study lounge. She'd lumber in there and prop three mirrors around her face on a large table. She'd lean in, run her finger along her widow's peak, and scowl. Her T-zone would shimmer under the overhead fluorescence. She'd raise tweezers to her hairline. They'd grab and pull.

Carmen stomped into our room.

"La pinche Yenifer está in the lounge plucking otra vez!" she whisper-shouted.

I set my book on my desk and tiptoed down the hall. I poked my head into the study area. There was Yenifer. That bitch was going to pluck herself cancer-patient smooth if she didn't stop. I returned to our triple.

"Yup," I said. "Mother plucker."

I made some instant Folgers. I read *History of the Franks*. I got up to pee. On my way to the john, I peeked into Yenifer's pluckateria.

She was still there, piles of hair littering the tabletop, tweezing the night away.

// //

Yenifer was standing by our window. She slid off her bandana.

"Ay, Yenifer! You're crazy!" said Carmen. "Look what you're doing to yourself!"

"I just want to get it straight!" Yenifer pointed at her hairline. Angelic rays hit her scalp. Her hairline had receded by about two inches. Recently plucked flesh pulsated.

"What should I do?" moaned Yenifer.

"Stop plucking!" we screamed.

// //

All day we practiced saying bye to each other. Thanksgiving break was upon us and Yenifer stood in our room saying a real good-bye. The rest of us were leaving tomorrow.

"Look," said Yenifer.

She slid back her bandana. Up sprang little black baby tufts, cubs ready to wrestle.

"Good job, Yenifer!" said Carmen.

"OK, hasta luego, you guys." Yenifer turned and left.

Carmen waited at the door, watching Yenifer wheel her suitcase to the elevator. Finally, Carmen declared, "She's gone!" and we got to work cracking each other up by imitating Yenifer for hours. We pretended to be gifted vocalists. We tugged at our hairlines.

Transcript of a 9-1-1 Call: November 15, 1996

DISPATCHER: 9-1-1 Emergency.

MALE VOICE: Yes, there is a lady being attacked on . . . the . . . Westside Little League park, by the snack bar, by two black girls . . . send help quick.

DISPATCHER: Wait, wait, wait, wait, wait, where, where is this park at?

MALE VOICE: It's Oakley, the Westside Little League . . .

DISPATCHER: Oakley Park?

MALE VOICE: Yes.

DISPATCHER: And is this the one off of Western? Or . . .

MALE VOICE: Yes, send help quick . . .

DISPATCHER: And they're beating her up?

MALE VOICE: Yes, they are. It's two black girls!

DISPATCHER: And they're in the baseball diamond?

MALE VOICE: Um, they're by the snack bar . . . and they're hitting her with the baseball bats and everything.

DISPATCHER: They're hitting her with baseball bats?

MALE VOICE: Yes.

DISPATCHER: Can you give me a description of these people?

MALE VOICE: Well, it's just two black girls, they're kinda heavyset.

DISPATCHER: Do you have any clothing description?

MALE VOICE: Um, no.

DISPATCHER: OK, you're calling from West Main. How come you went so far to call?

Male hung up the phone. Call ended.

Battered Body Found at School: Mysterious Phone Call Alerted the Authorities

Detectives have yet to turn up any suspects in a murder investigation stemming from the discovery of a woman's body Friday night next to the baseball field bleachers at Oakley School, the Santa Maria Police Department reported.

Police said they responded at 11 p.m. when a man called from the west side of town reporting a fight in progress at the North Western Avenue school.

When officers arrived at the scene, they discovered a woman lying on concrete behind the home-plate backstop fence, between the scorer's shack and the bleachers.

She died before officers arrived, police said, apparently from blunt-object injuries to the head, though a Monday autopsy will confirm the cause of her death.

The woman has tentatively been identified, but police said they are withholding her name until the next of kin are notified.

Saturday morning, police said they had few leads to go on.

There was a pool of blood on the ground and splattered blood on the scorer's shack set in the middle of perhaps two acres of grass.

The nearest house is roughly 100 yards away, and one curious boy, an onlooker who lives next to the park, said Saturday he and his family heard nothing until police arrived.

In fact, the mysterious telephone call reporting the "fight in progress" came from a pay phone "some distance away" from the park, according to Sgt. Dan Macagni.

The victim was described as a Latina woman, roughly 30 years old with brown hair and eyes. 5-foot-2-inches tall and weighing 130 pounds.

She was wearing a blue blouse and a black skirt.

Police urge those with information that could help the investigation to call 928-3781.

Burrito

I was home for Thanksgiving.

I sat in the rocking chair. The local news was on. An anchorwoman said that a transient had been bludgeoned to death next to Oakley School. The only lead was that two black girls might have done it.

"Bullshit," I thought. "That's total bullshit."

// //

December was cold in Berkeley and hella cold at 5 a.m.

That was when I'd get up to go to the gym. I'd pull on little boy's swim trunks, which I liked exercising in because of the built-in mesh underwear, and I'd stretch to prepare my muscles for pain. I'd sneak bites of the protein bars I'd stolen from Shakira and hidden in my desk. Well, I actually considered them borrowed. I planned on replacing them.

// //

I studied. I exercised. I studied. I exercised. I walked through the dark campus at night, knowing that squirrels and rapists prowled among the redwoods.

// //

Eating breakfast took too much time, so I gave up on power bars and cereal.

On an empty stomach, I laced up my Nikes and pulled on my sweatshirt. I jogged to the gym in my swim trunks while the sun rose. Its sterile atmosphere—polished walls, waxed floors, and white employees—soothed me.

This morning's crowd was thin, collectively and individually, and I climbed the second of six StairMasters facing a wall. On my machine I walked nowhere over and over again. I walked and ignored the queasiness multiplying in my cells. I ignored the weird fuzziness in my stomach.

I hiked through my discomfort, but my lips tingled. The StairMaster beeped. Its screen blinked, "Congratulations! Congratulations!" Digitized fireworks exploded across the control panel. It flashed how many calories I'd burned. Triple digits. I dismounted and pretended to feel fine. I headed to the weight room.

Only the diehards were there—men who worked on their physiques so hard they looked like flame-broiled chicken. A man whom I'd never seen smile was checking himself out in the mirror. He held two one-hundred-pound barbells and curled and grunted. His biceps bulged like sexy tumors, and his white goatee was like fleece against tobacco skin. His tight T-shirt announced, "The blacker the berry, the sweeter the juice."

I straddled a machine, reached, and pulled an overhead bar to the crook of my neck. I held the bar in place then released it slowly. I wanted to have He-Man's back. I pulled this weight down then released. I pulled this weight down then released. I let it go. A big uh-oh filled me. I tingled. My empty stomach was dying to say something.

The nurse came to mind. *You're going to have to get over this.*

I pulled the weight down again. I saw stars burst. I thought of our national anthem. I was going to have to contend with this. Something was about to happen.

I let the bar snap up. I stood and looked around.

No one noticed the warning signs.

I walked out of the weight room, down the hall, and into the ladies' room.

I knew what was coming. Perhaps you do too.

I lunged into a stall, yanked down my shorts, and bent over. A liquid laser shot out of me. The hotter it cut, the colder everywhere but my butthole felt. This burning stream confused me. I'd skipped dinner last night, and for lunch, I'd had an apple and peanut butter. Was I spraying residual shit? Was this something vestigial? My mind couldn't handle these questions. My head ached. I tried focusing on the burn. Eating it mentally. If you enter your pain instead of letting it enter you, you can eat it until it's gone. I think that's a tenet of Buddhism.

Sweat dripped from my face and into the toilet. I was melting. My T-shirt was damp and heavy. I spread my legs make-love-to-me-daddy wide and bowed my head. Peaches, browns, and golds swirled in the bowl. I was suffering from liquid impalement. I'd worked so hard to empty myself, and now here I sat, skewered by electrolyte imbalance.

I was going to pass out.

I slid my shorts up, unlocked the stall, and wobbled toward the sinks. I sank to the ground, and tile cooled my cheek. I wanted to absorb its coolness forever.

A lady screaming "Oh my god! OH MY GOD!" returned me to consciousness.

She left. She returned with reinforcements.

My hands and feet stiffened and twisted inward, lobster claws.

Fingers dug into my shorts pockets. They fished out my ID. I lifted an eyelid and watched a uniformed blonde kneel by the sink. She opened a first-aid kit.

I barfed.

It felt good.

A uniformed boy barged in. He snapped on a latex glove and unfurled an aluminum blanket on the floor. He rolled me onto it and rolled me up. Once I was fully wrapped, my bowels vacated.

"I am a bean burrito," I thought.

The girl who'd taken my ID said, "We called your roommate. She's on her way, so just hang in there."

I reached an arm out of my wrapper. In an I-heard-a-fly-buzz-when-I-died voice, I moaned, "I'm feeling better. I don't want to go in an ambulance."

"Are you epileptic?" asked the blonde. She held my wrist and took my pulse with her finger.

"I'm Mexican."

She stared at my face. "Your color is coming back."

I said, "I think I can stand."

"NO!" everybody screamed.

The guy who burritoed me wheeled in an office chair. "We're gonna help you into this," he said, grabbing my feet.

The blond girl reached under my armpits, and they heaved me onto the seat. The guy wheeled me out. He steered me past squash courts and rowing machines. In the lobby, we came to a stop and Carmen rushed toward me.

"For Christ's sake!" she screamed. "I thought I was coming to identify your body! This is really bad timing! I have an O chem test today."

"Sorry, I don't know what happened," I lied.

A woman wearing a name tag that read "supervisor" said, "Carmen, can you take your friend to the Tang Center?" That was our student health building.

"Yes," Carmen answered. "I'm premed." She walked around me. "How am I supposed to steer you? This chair doesn't have handles."

"Use my armpits," I said.

Carmen slid her hands in and murmured, "Warm."

She pushed me outside and navigated me down Bancroft's sloping sidewalk. She wheeled me into the Tang Center, where I sat on an examination table and a nurse practitioner fed me stale crackers and apple juice. As I chewed and sipped, she wrote me a prescription, tore it off her pad, and handed it to me.

I held it in front of my face and read its simple, familiar prescription: "Eat."

The Albatross

The best part of Christmas is getting up before everyone else and un-wrapping their presents, but that part hadn't come yet, only the vaca-tion part had. I was at my parents', balancing my time between reading for pleasure and running laps around our neighborhood. Tendinitis had taken up residence in my hips, but that didn't stop me. I looked forward to arthritis.

Sunday night was spaghetti night, and I'd eaten a little serving of it. Tomato sauce hardened on the dishes sitting in the sink. We piled onto the couches. The TV was on.

"More news on the murder of the transient who was raped and beaten to death near Oakley School this November," said the announcer. "Police now have a suspect: this man." His face appeared onscreen. "He's also suspected in several other attacks against local women."

With my mouth open, I stared at his mug shot. It was unassuming, nothing diabolical about it. His expression seemed just a little bit sur-prised, but I'd seen it look sadistically joyful. That face. It bobbed for apples between my thighs. It wore my crotch. Those nostrils huffed my fear. His smile undressed me, bent me over, and exposed me to planet Earth and all her gentle creatures.

"That's him," I said.

Herman, Ofelia, Mom, and Dad stared at the man who'd seen parts of me in ways they never will. They said nothing.

// //

I was on the phone with Detective Lopez. "Have you seen the news?" he asked.

"Yes."

"Then you know why I'm calling."

"Yes."

"Is it him?"

"Yes."

"Thank you. You'll be hearing from the district attorney soon."

"Bye."

I hung up. I walked outside. I ran.

// //

I was killing time at our piano bench, striking keys, creating "experimental music." A bust of Aphrodite, carved from marble, sat atop the instrument. She stared through my head, white eyes focused on the Christmas tree behind me.

The tree's lights were off. Overzealous ornamentation made its arms sag. An angel crowned it. She was white, unlike our nativity set's constituents. Since our nativity set came from Mexico, its holy family, angels, magi, and livestock (there was even a turkey) were indigenous. Aztec Jesus rested in an Aztec cradle on our walnut credenza, a pretty baby born for the sake of human sacrifice.

Outside, clouds turned the sky to gravy. Gloom pressed against the tall living room windows. White carpet couldn't brighten the mood, and neither could the beige couches. The Christmas tree and baby Jesus were trying to make things cheerful, but the shitty weather trumped them.

Someone knocked at the front door. I kept playing.

They knocked harder. They rang the doorbell.

Mom's head appeared beside Aphrodite's. She walked the parquet floor, peeped through the stained-glass doorframe, and reached for the lock. Whoever it was must've looked safe. She unlocked the door and opened it.

"Hello?"

My fingers rested on white keys. I heard a man ask if this was my residence.

"Yes," answered Mom.

"Here," said the man. "She's been served."

The piano blocked my view of the hand foisting papers through our doorway. It blocked my view of Mom accepting my subpoena. (How humiliating to get raped and then served with a subpoena. Couldn't they call it something less violating or phallic?)

I listened to the man whistling as he left our brick porch.

I watched him walk the concrete path lined with diseased rose bushes. We'd inherited these from the house's previous owners, a frugal rocket scientist and his wife. The rocket scientist had worked for NASA and jerry-rigged many things in our house with paper clips and rubber cement. His handiwork was constantly breaking down.

"No wonder the *Challenger* blew up," Dad would say as he repaired another one of the rocketeer's quick fixes.

Mom shut the door. She turned toward me, her face poised beside Aphrodite's.

I shook my head.

She showed me she loved me by making my subpoena disappear.

// //

Two ideas swam circles around each other like sharks in the aquarium of my skull.

Shark One was made up of this logic: The timing of the attacks, as reported by the news, made me first. If he'd killed her around Thanksgiving and attacked the others, THE OTHERS, that fall and December, then I could've stopped him. If I'd chased him into that alley, caught up to him, taken off my shoe, and beaten him with it like Mom taught me you're supposed to do with cockroaches, then he wouldn't have been out stalking, grabbing, and mutilating women. He might've turned around and killed me, but that would have been OK. Then I wouldn't be living with this guilt. This guilt was an invisible but heavy albatross hanging around my neck. (That's a reference to Coleridge's *The Rime of the Ancient Mariner*.) I wear that bird like Björk wore her swan dress. I wave from a red carpet leading to hell.

A different series of propositions made up Shark Two: Let's say I did testify against him. Let's say I cried during my testimony. Let's say after that I went to law school and became a lawyer. Let's say I tried to find work in the local courthouse where my case got tried. Let's say the judges and attorneys and clerks and bailiffs who worked there when I testified went on to work there forever. That's what happens in small towns—people work in the same place forever. Let's say I got invited to interview for a job there and when people saw me in my suit, holding a briefcase, waiting, they remembered me. Let's say they remembered me as the girl who took the witness stand and cried when she described getting grabbed and having things put where they didn't belong. Could the employees of this courthouse ever take me seriously as a litigator? As a superior? As an officer of the court?

No way.

I'd be that girl that got raped by that cholo just like the boys Mr. Osmond fucked are still referred to as the boys Mr. Osmond fucked.

DEPARTMENT OF CORRECTIONS AND REHABILITATION
DIVISION OF ADULT OPERATIONS

Death Row Tracking System
Condemned Inmate List (Secure)

Last Name	First Name	Age	Age at Offense
MARENTES	DESI	38	28
MARKS	DELANEY	60	34
MARLOW	JAMES	60	30
			30
MARTIN	VALERIE	49	36
MARTINEZ	TOMMY	39	19
MARTINEZ	MICHAEL	50	25
MARTINEZ	OMAR	56	28
MARTINEZ	CARLOS	40	30
MARTINEZ	SANTIAGO	35	22
MARTINEZ	ALBERTO	38	24
MASTERS	JARVIS	54	23
MATAELE	TUPOUTOE	44	25
MAURY	ROBERT	58	27
MCCLAIN	HERBERT	48	25
MCCURDY	GENE	56	37
MCDANIEL	DONTE	36	25
			24
MCDERMOTT	MAUREEN	69	38
MCDOWELL	CHARLES	63	29
MCGHEE	TIMOTHY	43	24
			28
			27
MCKINNON	CRANDALL	49	27
MCKINZIE	KENNETH	57	41
MCKNIGHT	ANTHONY	63	32

Spring Semester 1997

// //

I still believed I could lose myself in homework and exercise.

Motivated by this creed, I put on my little boy's swim trunks and Nikes. I grabbed my Walkman, this ancient device that played cassettes or enabled you to listen to the radio, and headed outside.

The day was gray. I jogged along College Avenue, toward Rockridge. Mozart jogged with me.

Mozart is the sound of civilization and its decline.

We sprinted past bungalows, a laundromat, and the Catholic church that looked like a Soviet-era construction. Trees had shed large leaves you could have swaddled a baby in. They gave the sidewalk bedding. If, from behind, someone struck me with a bat, the leaves would have cushioned my fall.

In front of a two-story house with a menorah large enough for a crucifixion on the lawn, invisible arms encircled my waist. They held me.

I stopped, half-expecting my pants to be pulled down.

I turned around.

No one was there.

My finger rolled along the volume dial, turning it up.

I took a step and another and I was jogging, but the hands, which I knew were not real, returned. I ripped off my headphones and spun around.

The memory of him wanted to run with me.

I wanted to run with Mozart.

// //

My History of Modern Europe class was so full I had to sit on the floor at the top of the auditorium. I pressed my back to the wall and tucked my knees against my chest.

The doors were shoved open. A cartoonish Asian girl wearing a heavy cat eye, frosted bouffant, and chunky heels clomped in. As she swung past me, I saw up her blue skirt. Smooth thighs and a garter belt. Like William Blake, I experienced a vision: me lunging at her and sinking my fingers into her bouffant then pounding her skull into the steps. Her brains dripped down them.

// //

My modern Europe TA stuck a happy-face sticker to the paper I wrote on *The Prince*. Underneath the sticker, he wrote, "An insightful piece of work, but one question: Do you *really* think Camille Paglia is a direct descendant of Machiavelli?"

// //

An unfamiliar discomfort woke me.

Maybe my bladder was full. Maybe this sensation was that old feeling being translated into new body language. I labeled the weirdness *having to pee,* got out of bed, and tiptoed out of our triple.

I stepped into the bathroom. It smelled of farts and perfume, which reminded me of my mother.

Sitting on the toilet, I squeezed. I squeezed and squeezed and wrung a single tear from my urethra. No reason to flush or wipe.

I walked back to our triple and climbed into bed.

Our dorm was quiet.

The sensation of his pressing remained.

// //

His face tried to cuddle between my legs. His chin tapped my bladder, digging. I peed to get rid of him, but he drank these repellent/resplendent showers. His ghost, his memory, was thirsty.

We sat in Yenifer's room. I was helping her study for a linguistics final.

"*Ain't* ain't a word," I said. "Uh-huh. Uh-huh. Those are glottal stops, I think. Do one. Uh-oh."

"Uh-oh," Yenifer repeated.

Peruvian music was playing on her ghetto blaster. That's what she called it. She pointed at it with one red fingernail and said, in her deep, creepy Chicana voice, "I touch myself to Peruvian music." An Incan wailed a solo on pan pipes. Wind chimes tinkled. Yenifer licked her lips and adjusted her headband. She added, "Sometimes, when I touch myself, I feel the spirits of my ancestors."

I wasn't sure what to say.

Yenifer asked, "What music do you touch yourself to?"

"I don't," I confessed.

"Do you want me to loan you a Peruvian CD?"

"No, thanks," I said. Even though she had confided something intimate to me, I was not about to tell Yenifer that when I was little I'd taken my temperature to *The Diary of Anne Frank.*

The Other Women

I ran to the phone mounted between our family room and kitchen. I was home for spring break and looking forward to harming marshmallow Peeps.

"Hello?"

"Hello, may I please speak to Myriam Gurba?"

"This is she."

"Hi. This is district attorney Nathaniel Garcia." He paused. "I need to ask you some questions about what happened to you on July 22."

Fish twisted in my stomach. "All right." I sat on an oak stool.

"Can you please walk me through what happened?"

I inhaled. I said, "I'm walking up the street, on my way to my mom's school and . . ." I relived what happened from a casual observer's point of view, a bird looking down from a wire. I stayed present tense in my narration.

DA Garcia coughed. In an uncomfortable but impressed tone, he said, "Thank you. That's exactly what you told the detective. Exactly. Thank you." He paused. "If you're interested, I can put you in touch with a counselor who works with victims like you. She's very good. The other women have been seeing her."

The other woman. The other women. Kept women. *Little Women.* D. H. Lawrence's *Women in Love.* Gudrun. Ursula. Women Seeking Women.

"Thanks, but I go to school really far away. I don't live here anymore."

"OK. Well, here's her number, just in case."

DA Garcia dictated it. I cracked my knuckles while staring at a bowl of seedless grapes.

// //

I blew off DA Garcia's other calls.

I was not going to go down in local history as the girl who was weirdly raped by the Mexican guy who murdered the lady in the park. I had medieval history to learn.

Summer Session 1997

// //

I moved into a one-bedroom apartment on Dwight Way and spent my summer taking one class, dying my hair, and telemarketing. The telemarketing was paid fundraising for my school, and I greeted alumni with this shtick: "You'll never guess who's calling!"

After the alumnus on the other end of the line named the child they'd given up for adoption or a long-lost lover, I'd declare, "No! It's Myriam Gurba! From the Cal Annual Fund! Do you have your checkbook handy?"

I gloated that summer, too. I could set personal goals and meet them. I'd already become buff and gotten my 4.00, so I gave myself a new challenge: to have sex with a married man. It seemed like a good idea to have sex with someone and ruin his family. I wanted to see whether or not my pussy had the mettle for this. Males had co-opted my genitalia to prove their destructive powers, and I felt it was time to reclaim their destructive powers for my own use.

The married man I set my sights on was my professor. He was youngish, blond, and handsome (by Berkeley standards). He often mentioned his new baby, so I guessed he hadn't had sex in a while. He held his office hours in Dwinelle Hall.

I dressed strategically for these in extra small T-shirts, rubber or animal-print miniskirts, and pumps. I sat near him, gauging his temperature. His widening pit stains and pink cheeks told me I had an effect. He stroked his tie clip. His foot tapped the tile. These were not the moves I was looking for. I had wanted him to bust the moves.

He was basing half our grade on a big-ass paper, and I was considering writing mine about German interwar perverts. While we were studying together at a café, Ruth told me she had a drama professor who might serve as an intellectual resource for this endeavor. He was an expert on Weimar culture and super into Anita Berber, the dykey drug addict who danced nude and became the subject of that ugly/extremely sexy Otto Dix painting.

"Is he gay?" I asked.

"He's the opposite of gay."

"Is he married?"

"He lives with an ex-lesbian."

"This could work," I thought.

Before work, I walked to the drama department and slid a note with my phone number into the professor's mailbox. He called. We agreed to meet at a café near the Julia Morgan pool. I showed up in a lace slip and ordered a cappuccino. He paid. My moustache sipped foam. He leered.

I was having an effect.

"Would you like to meet again, my dear?" he asked when our half-hour conversation was up. "I can help you write an amazing paper." He smirked and adjusted himself. Ruth had warned me he had a penile implant.

"ok."

"Call me, my dear," he said, winking.

// //

I called him.

// //

The professor picked me up in a Dodge and drove me to a Mediterranean restaurant in Elmwood. A waitress seated us at a sidewalk table. She brought us wine, dolmas, olives, and lamb shanks on beds of rice. Behind the professor, a movie marquee advertised a French film.

"Want to see that movie when we're done?" I asked.

He turned, read the title, and turned back. "French cinema is shit," he spat.

I laughed. Wine stained my teeth, tongue, and uvula. Wine pickled me.

"Those pompous movies don't appeal to basic human nature," said the professor.

"What movies do?" I slurred.

"Rambo."

Rimbaud.

He poured me more wine. He talked. He was a talker. I sized him up as I let him prattle. Men like it if you let them talk. It makes them feel like teachers. That's all many men really want. To be womankind's teacher.

The professor was slight. He had a Sally Field build and dark hair. Gray roots showed at his part—he must've dyed. Hound-dog jowls framed his mouth. He wore rimless glasses, a long-sleeved black shirt, and black slacks. Typical. I ignored my lamb, picked almonds from the rice, and finished the wine.

I hiccupped, "So we're not going to the movie?"

"I'll take you to see that piece of shit if you want."

He took out his wallet and set cash on the table. We got up. Diners stared. I was purple haired, hairy, wobbly, and dressed in lingerie. Steering me by the elbow, the professor led me to the theatre's awning. He bought two tickets from a box-office girl reading the Bhagavad Gita. He hustled me past the concession stand faster than anyone could say *extra butter.*

Guiding me into the dark cinema, he pulled me to the back row. I fell into a seat. He sat beside me. He jammed his hand into my crotch. He grabbed my bush as if it were balls.

"Is this what you want?" he asked.

I nodded. On screen, a little girl with pigtails rode a swing.

"I hate French cinema," he said through clenched teeth. He rubbed me vengefully.

"Then why don't we leave?" I asked.

"Really?"

"Yeah. I don't want to watch a little Belgian girl swing while you finger me. That's sick."

A lady a couple rows up turned around and glared.

I got up and he steered me out. We walked up College Avenue. He whispered filthy words in my ear, how my ginormous cunt was drooling special-edishly for him, etcetera, etcetera, and I concentrated on not tripping. He paused at the mouth of an alley.

He let go of me and walked into it.

I wasn't going to chicken out this time. I followed the nebbish behind a dumpster.

"Against the wall," he said.

I leaned and trembled. He reached up my slip, fingered me, wiped his hand down my bare back, and said, "You've just been diddled by a Jew. How does it feel?"

"Kosher . . ." I whispered.

Fall Semester 1997

HISTORY 4B
HISTORY 141A
HISTORY 166A
WOMENST 102
WOMENST 198

// //

Yeah, history class was where I got molested. Nonetheless, I couldn't stop taking history classes.

I really love history.

// //

Everything has a history.

// //

Even doorknobs have a history.

// //

I stopped bleaching my moustache.

I had sex with one more guy—he looked a little like Hugh Grant—and then my pussy became the Michigan Womyn's Festival. Every night was ladies' night.

I got a cowboy hat.

In overalls, Converse, and a leopard-print bra, I BARTed to San Francisco. I wandered through Chinatown, past City Lights Books, and into North Beach. I walked into the first strip club I saw. I sat at the tip rail. A guy and I watched a skin-and-bones stripper crawl toward us.

"Are you looking for a job?" she asked me as she shook her long nipples in my face.

"No," I said. "I'm looking for you." Strobe lights flashed. She may have blushed. She breathed in. I asked, "Can I buy a dance?"

She nodded.

I stood. She climbed off the rail and led me toward the shadowy rear of the club, to a private booth. Once I was inside with her, she pulled the curtain shut behind us. She delicately pushed me down on a tiny bench. Facing me, she stepped onto the bench, climbed up, straddled my face, and spread her legs above my eyes. Her genitals became my tiara and both of us froze. The stripper was me and I was him. I was reenacting the history of that moment after the art museum from a different perspective.

Spring Semester 1998

ENGLISH 117T

HISTORY 103B

HISTORY 150C

PHYSICS 10

// //

DELIBERATIONS UNDER WAY IN MARTINEZ MURDER TRIAL

A jury of eight women and four men began deliberations at 3 p.m. Tuesday on the fate of Tommy Jesse Martinez Jr. and is scheduled to resume this morning.

Martinez, 20, is accused of murder in the rape, stabbing, and bludgeoning death of 35-year-old Sophia Castro Torres in a Santa Maria park on Nov. 15, 1996.

He is also accused of three other incidents, including attempted assaults against other Santa Maria women from Nov. 3 until Dec. 4, 1996. He has confessed to attempted robbery and assault in two of these incidents, including the latter, after which Santa Maria police nabbed him.

He has denied charges of attempted rape and one count each of kidnapping and attempted kidnapping.

The jury can work until 5 p.m. nightly until it makes its decisions, according to instructions from Superior Court Judge Rodney Melville.

The trial began May 19, after a week spent in jury selection.

District Attorney Tom Sneddon and assistant prosecutor Tracy Grossman have asked the jury to find Martinez guilty of first-degree murder. Sneddon announced months ago he would seek the death penalty.

If the jury does find Martinez guilty of first-degree murder, the trial will go into a penalty phase. Melville said this second phase would begin immediately after such a decision.

During closing arguments Tuesday morning, defense attorney Peter Dullea urged the jury to look at the "reasonable doubt" on the basis of circumstantial evidence without the "loaded emotional phrases" offered by Sneddon.

Much of this evidence has two possibilities for interpretation, he claimed.

Evidence, including DNA, *shows that Martinez had sexual intercourse with Torres before her death.*

Earlier testimony showed that Torres had been profoundly depressed, isolated, and dysfunctional.

Although she appeared quite reclusive, Dullea suggested that she sought release from her emotional pain not with drugs or alcohol, but by finding warmth in the arms of a stranger.

"People do things like that," he added.

// //

Warmth in the arms of a stranger. Wow.

// //

German Jewish toker, hiker, and intellectual Walter Benjamin wrote an essay titled "Unpacking My Library: A Talk about Book Collecting." In it, he describes his musty zeal, intoning that "every passion borders on the chaotic, but the collector's passion borders on the chaos of memories." The chaos of memories. The chaos of mammaries. That chaos that comes after being touched. The chaos of penetration. That chaos of breath. The chaos caused by quiet ghosts. The haunting.

Fall Semester 1998

CHICANO 198

HISTORY 103E

HISTORY 171A

SCANDIN 116

// //

I really like the phrase "the chaos of memories." My spirit latches onto it and wraps its arms around its queer, hairy legs. The phrase expresses what kind of happens to your brain during and after trauma. Chaos roots itself in memory. My chaos came when a Mexican man sexually assaulted me on a sidewalk in the afternoon sun. Birds watched and kept the story to themselves. I told a detective about it, but I didn't tell him everything. Some parts felt too personal for the historical record. Some of my reality wanted to, and wants to, remain private. By denying certain events a place in the historical record, there's a certain denial of truth. With that denial comes dignity. Belief in one's basic dignity is like makeup. It helps you leave the house. It protects your real face, the you-est you, against judgments.

Sometimes, it's best to protect what the arms, faces, fingers, and mouths of strangers have done to you from misinterpretation. Like a chipmunk, I hoard the memory of all the sensations that happened to me that afternoon by the railroad tracks. I invite some people to experience parts of the assemblage.

Like Benjamin, I am a collector.

Spring Semester 1999

ANTHRO C147B

CHICANO 198

HISTORY 101

WOMENST 199

// //

I could tell you about meeting my wife, our courtship, and our relationship, but I'm not going to. This is not a coming-out story. This is not a romance novel. As René Magritte would say, "Ceci n'est pas that kind of thing." As Gertrude Stein would say, "There is no there there." As Kimberly "Sweet Brown" Wilkins would say, "Ain't nobody got time for that."

Fall Semester 1999

HISTORY H102
HISTORY H195

// //

I graduated cum laude with a history degree. I think I minored in women's studies. History is the place where I got molested. History made me cum laude.

The Return of Elizabitch

I rarely let myself think about Sophia. In fact, I never let myself think about Sophia.

My brain, though, *wanted* to think about her.

My brain was *obsessed* with her.

It sought a surrogate.

It chose the Black Dahlia.

I came across her in a book subtitled "An Illustrated History of the Los Angeles County Department of the Coroner." I ogled the book's black-and-white photographs of her pre and post mutilation. They joined the chaos in my brain and fused with my memories of the human sacrifice at Oakley Park.

After staring at her crime scene and autopsy photos, I thought about the Black Dahlia all the time. I thought about her while I pooped. I thought about her while I ran. I thought about her while I ate fried chicken. I thought about her while I cut my bangs. She'd been a pretty white girl, the depressed kind, my *favorite* kind. Then somebody molested her, tortured her, chopped her up, and dumped her in a weedy lot. Los Angeles went nuts over her lust murder because she'd been so pretty, so white, and now she was in pieces. Who could do this to such a pretty white girl? Apparently, somebody. Pretty white girls needed to be careful. Pretty white girls needed to stay home.

1947 was the Black Dahlia's big year.

She became famous for being lifeless, pretty, and white.

Dad was born in 1947.

He is part white. The Black Dahlia was white in parts. Two. Her killer bisected her at the waist. He also etched a smile into her face that extended her natural mouth beyond its perimeters. Sophia's face got cut too. He never threatened to cut my face, but he threatened to cut other girls. He told them he wanted to cut their pretty faces. He breathed on them. His breath smelled like peanuts and chocolate. He smiled and smiled. He wrote poetry and he murdered. He cut, beat, and came. Cum laude.

// //

The Black Dahlia's real name was Elizabeth Short.
 Elizabitch.
 Elizabitch.
 Elizabitch.

The Collector

Mexicans are naturally inclined to steal. I succumbed to this natural inclination at an Oakland cemetery.

I'd convinced my friend, a chain-smoking gay named Bob, to drive me there so we could visit the Black Dahlia's grave. We stared down at its dirt.

I didn't realize that I was staring at my Sophia surrogate. But I was.

"What's the point of this?" asked Bob.

I looked left. I looked right. I pulled a plastic sandwich bag out of my jeans pocket, knelt, and clawed at the dirt. I scooped it into the bag. (This was premeditated.)

Bob said, "I don't think that's a very good idea. What if you piss her off?"

"She can't get pissed," I said. "She's dead."

Bob chuckled. He ashed on the cemetery dirt.

// //

This is not a love story, but I must discuss the white girl I mentioned earlier, the white girl who would go on to become my wife, a white girl I met in college. She was my favorite kind of white girl, the depressed kind who gets chased out of bathrooms for looking like a boy, the kind who has suffered and suffered and suffered, and one day, I would say "I do" to her.

We were living together in Berkeley, but I talked her into moving south with me to Long Beach.

The Black Dahlia had lived there.

// //

Bob moved to Long Beach with us.

He slept on our living room floor.

He went out at night to get his dick sucked.

In our neighborhood, it was easy to get your dick sucked.

In the moonlight.

One morning, I found Bob sitting on the living room floor eating a cold cheeseburger.

"Good morning," I said to him. "Did you have any disgusting adventures last night?"

Bob was usually giggly, but he didn't giggle. He set his cheeseburger down on the floor. He looked up at me and said, "I saw her."

"Who?" I asked.

"The Black Dahlia," he said.

"What? Where?"

Bob explained how he'd gone to the bars, had some drinks, wandered home, and crashed on the floor. He woke up at some point, probably in the early morning, and saw a black-haired woman walking through the living room. "I thought it was you," he said. "But then she turned to look at me. She looked at me over her shoulder. When she showed her face, it wasn't you. It was her."

I got quiet and probably pale.

I had to get rid of that dirt.

The Post-traumatic Bitch and the Sea

My girlfriend was at work and Bob was on a date.

It was perfect. It was nighttime and I was alone.

I approached my jewelry box. The same one I'd kept acid in as a teen. I opened its lid. The ballerina didn't spin. I reached for the plastic baggy and shoved it in my sweatshirt pocket.

I left our apartment, headed through our courtyard, and made my way past the gay bars. The gayborhood smelled of wine and precum. Stars twinkled.

I marched the few blocks to the concrete stairs that cut down a cliff. I headed down to the beach and padded across its darkness, to the tide.

At the edge of the dry earth, I pulled the bag out of my pocket. I untwisted it, turned it over, and let sand sprinkle into sea.

The sea took it.

I dropped the bag in, too.

I wanted all of it to go back to the sea even though I hadn't stolen it from the sea.

I wasn't only trying to get rid of the Dahlia.

I was trying to free myself from the other ghost, too.

Jobs

I worked as a receptionist.

// //

I worked reading books to the blind.

// //

I worked as an artist's model. You don't have to be pretty to do that.

// //

I got a job teaching history.

Doing Donuts

I was checking out the merchandise at a donut shop.

It was the kind that sells novelties. They had dick donuts, bacon donuts, donuts covered in different sugary cereals, and post-mortem pastries filled with jelly. One donut caught my eye. Its laminated label read, "The Michael Jackson: a chocolate cake donut covered in white powdered sugar."

The people I was hanging out with launched into a debate about whether or not this donut was racist. Was the creation of this donut a racist act? Was this donut an act of violence? This was the only time in my life I've heard the words *hegemony* and *donut* used in the same sentence.

What I found most interesting wasn't the debate about the racial implications of this donut. What I found most interesting was that everybody dominating this debate was white. The two of us listening to this debate, the two of us whose opinions were never solicited, looked at one another. We locked eyes. We were the only two mud people there.

// //

I don't know if Michael Jackson molested kids. I don't know if the Michael Jackson donut molested kids.

I know he *really* liked being around kids and shared his bed with them, which is weird. Come on, it's weird.

// //

I really like his music.

// //

I was on the phone with Dad.

I called him and Mom every Sunday. Our conversations usually lasted about half an hour. Dad was yammering. He would not shut up about Michael Jackson.

His molestation trial had recently begun in the courthouse down the street from Dad's work, the same one where the trial I'd been asked to testify in happened.

The judge who presided over Michael Jackson's trial, Judge Melville, was the same judge who presided over Sophia's.

I went to high school with Judge Melville's daughter. She was a cheerleader. Everybody joked that she walked the way she did because her boyfriend liked to stick his huge dick up her butt. There might have been some truth in this.

Jackson's prosecutor, Sneddon, was the same prosecutor who argued that Tommy Jesse Martinez Jr. was indeed a rapist, a murderer, and terrorizer of women.

I chose not to testify against him.

I did not want to see the other women.

I did not want to see his face.

And Ofelia tried killing herself the day after I got subpoenaed. I didn't mention that earlier because I wasn't sure if I wanted it to be part of the historical record. I wasn't sure how detailed I wanted to be regarding dead and dying girls overwhelming me that winter. I ran from them, but dead and dying girls have a way of taking up vivid residence in the post-traumatic brain.

It was weird watching people get famous through Michael Jackson's body. It was weird watching people get famous through sick boys' bodies. They never would've gotten so famous through a dead strawberry picker's body. Through a Mexican woman's semen-stained corpse.

Sophia had regularly eaten lunch at the Salvation Army across the street from the courthouse. Paparazzi now besieged it.

"There's actually traffic! Traffic!" Dad cried in disbelief. "It's pandemonium. I'm not joking. I can't even walk to the mall for lunch. I tried walking up the street to go to the mall, and you know what I saw?"

"What?"

"Somebody dressed as a giant panda. It was on roller skates."

"A Michael Jackson supporter?"

"No. It was handing out coupons to Panda Express."

"Did you take one?"

"No. I prefer Pick Up Stix."

"Oh."

// //

The trial's most infamous moment didn't happen in the courtroom; it happened in the parking lot.

Michael Jackson hopped onto a car. A sea of fans engulfed it. Michael Jackson waved at them, reaching out to hold hands with a few. Voices chanted, "Michael! Michael!" His music played. Fans cheered from the sidewalks Sophia had walked down glumly.

// //

When his not-guilty verdict was announced, some crazy bitch released doves into the air outside the courthouse. They flew over the parking lot, over the Salvation Army, and into the sun.

Capital Murder

I got picked to go to Washington, DC.

I went with a bunch of other teachers from around the country to learn about the Supreme Court. This was supposed to make us better history teachers. We were going to get to be where judicial history was and is made. We were going to get to touch it. I didn't want it to touch me back. I'm usually not a tactile learner.

// //

We milled around in a room in the Supreme Court building. A handler was arranging us, posing us around the seventeenth chief justice of the Supreme Court, the Honorable John G. Roberts. The handler grabbed my elbow and shoved me next to him. Other petite teachers were propped close to him, too, and with those of slight stature surrounding him, an optical illusion emerged. Roberts no longer appeared elfin. He looked tall.

"Oh my god," I thought. "He's the Court's Tom Cruise. He's fucking short."

"Cheese!" we shouted in the tastefully conservative reception room. Cherrywood paneling bedecked by portraits of jurists the average American probably can't identify surrounded us. This meet-and-greet with an actual justice, this jurisprudential petting zoo moment, was supposed to be the highlight of three days' worth of sandwiches, pizzas, roundtable talks, lectures, and PowerPoints from journalists, wonks, law professors, historians, bloggers, and the like.

Roberts showed up fifteen minutes late.

And to be honest, I was disappointed. I hadn't wanted to meet the chief justice. I'd wanted to meet Clarence Thomas.

I'd come prepared to meet him.

I was going to ask him to split a Coke with me.

// //

"It's a hoax," I said.

We were stepping out of a makeshift dining room where teachers had just torn apart an Italian buffet. The teacher from Detroit was staring at her phone.

"Well," she said. "That's what the text says. Michael Jackson's dead."

// //

Back at the hotel, in a room I was sharing with Dorothy, a teacher from South Carolina, we watched CNN.

News anchors were narrating what they suspected Michael Jackson's last minutes were like. They described his thin, dead body. I pictured it as a Cheeto with vitiligo.

Dorothy's phone rang. She answered. In her Southern drawl, she squealed, "We're watchin' the news about Michael Jackson!"

Seconds passed. Dorothy laughed. She turned to me. "Wanna hear a joke about Michael Jackson?" she asked.

I wondered if the joke would be racist, homophobic, transphobic, or a triple threat.

"Fine," I said.

Dorothy rushed through the telling in a guilty voice. The punch line: Little Boy Blew.

"Didn't you say you were a preacher's wife?" I asked her.

She nodded and returned to her conversation with her son.

Lying on my bed on my stomach, I listened to the news. Commentators kept saying it was the end of an era. It didn't feel that way. It didn't feel real. Mr. Osmond was still alive and Michael Jackson lived through him. Mr. Osmond *was* Michael Jackson. Tommy *was* Michael Jackson. Michael Jackson *was* my childhood. Michael Jackson *was* my innocence before I knew what innocence was. Michael Jackson *was* my mother and father. Michael Jackson *was* my sister. Michael Jackson was not my brother but he would've loved my brother. Michael Jackson *was* my skin. Michael Jackson *was* my thighs. Michael Jackson *was* confusion. Michael Jackson *was* virginity. Michael Jackson *was* my country. Michael Jackson *was* the white knight of my soul and the dark night of my soul and the dark light of my soul and, most of all, Michael Jackson was a donut.

Michael Jackson was now another racially ambiguous corpse. As a racially ambiguous living person, he'd been tried in a courtroom presided over by the whitest of judges. A Melville. He got Moby Dicked.

I wondered about Michael Jackson's dying. I wondered about Michael Jackson dying his skin. The idea of his corpse moved me. All racially ambiguous bodies move me. They feel close. Like family. The dead are still our family.

// //

On this historic evening, I revealed my connection to Michael Jackson to Dorothy.

"You know how Michael Jackson got tried for molesting kids?" I began. "Well, that happened in my hometown. The judge who was in charge of his trial presided over a trial I was supposed to be a part of."

"Really?"

"Yeah. When I was nineteen, I sort of got raped."

Dorothy was trying to think of something nice to say. She leaned against her elbows, faced me from her bed, and said, "Maybe he couldn't help himself because you're so gorgeous."

I thought about all the ugly people who get raped. Was I one of them?

"I don't think so," I said.

Dorothy was quiet for a little while. Eventually, she asked, "Why didn't you go to the trial?"

"I was embarrassed," I said. "And I felt guilty about being alive. The guy who attacked me attacked other women too. One got her head smashed. She died."

Hugging my pillow, I looked at our nightstand. Michael Jackson's ghost was in everything.

"My son's in federal prison . . ." Dorothy began. She tried to console me with an account of her imperfections as a mother and the sinful ways of those she'd parented.

// //

Justice Thomas sat at the highest bench in the land, staring at the ceiling. Besides sexually harassing Anita Hill, that's what he's most notorious for—being the quietest and weirdest Supreme Court justice in American history. The judge who stares at the crown molding and says nothing during arguments.

I sat in the audience with the other teachers, watching Justice Scalia read a majority opinion. Nearby, Justice Ginsburg rolled her eyes.

Justice Thomas leaned back in his chair. A mug of something devoid of pubic hair rested in front of him. The ceiling's corners fascinated him. His mind was so far away.

Was he thinking about Michael Jackson?

// //

I jogged in Washington, DC. I jogged and jogged and jogged. I jogged to the Library of Congress. I jogged to its walls and I leaned against them and I touched them and I touched them and I touched them.

Flower Girl

Have you ever made a pilgrimage in a Chrysler?

I have.

When I went home for Thanksgiving, we rode to Oakley Park as a family. I'd anticipated squeezing a catharsis out of this pilgrimage, but I should've known my dreams of closure would remain dreams. I was traveling to the park with Mexicans, and Mexicans ruin everything except grass. I'm Mexican, so I'm ruined. My mom is Mexican and, thus, she gave birth to my ruin. My dad is half Mexican, which is the same as all Mexican. My white girlfriend, the mannish woman I married, came with us.

The night she met me, after I told her I was Mexican, she announced, "I love Selena."

"The president of her fan club shot her," I said.

We danced.

Dad's PT Cruiser coasted to a stop at Oakley Park's curb. Dad parallel parked. The engine quieted. Dad's hands stayed on the wheel. He didn't unbuckle his seatbelt.

"Are you coming?" I asked.

He shook his comb-over. What a dick.

I didn't think of him as a pussy—he hadn't earned that compliment. He was huddling in the driver's seat to avoid gory memories. What's more familiar with gore than the pussy, the vadge, the bivalve, the clam? All gore originates from this blind sea creature, this moist, briny, hungry anemone. Every day, she belches fresh tales of life, death, and every weird thing in between. Chorizo can't compete.

My girlfriend and I climbed out of the backseat. Mom climbed out the passenger-side door. The three of us walked the landing strip of grass between curb and sidewalk. We crossed into the park. I watched my girlfriend lunge at a palm tree. She clung to its ashy shaft. She smiled an apology.

"You're not gonna come?" I asked.

Desperation strained my *come*?

"Go," she urged. My girlfriend slid her phone from her pocket. She fingered it. (Did junior high ruin that word for you too?)

A Yoda-like inner voice addressed me: "Patient with your girlfriend and your father be . . ."

Maybe this was a hard thing for my family to do. To come to this place with me. We were here at the urging of my therapist. So far, she had been my best therapist. She hadn't fallen asleep on me. Yet.

I smiled at my girlfriend, giving her permission to stay. I turned. I stared at the park's lawn. I thought of the Mexicans who probably tended it.

I lifted my foot and brought it down. My shoe crushed a dandelion. It wept cheerful milk. Together, Mom and I entered the grass. We meandered this way and that way and this way and that way and that way and another way and this way and that way and this way and that way and this way and that way and this way and that way.

Mom muttered, "P'aquí, p'allá, p'aquí p'aquí, p'aquí, p'allá, p'aquí, p'allá . . . parecemos gitanos," which translates to "This way, that way, this way, that way . . . we look like Gypsies." (It's not PC, but that's what she said.)

She asked, "Adónde quieres ir, m'ija?" "Where do you want to go, my daughter?"

"I don't know."

I almost added, "Where they found her body," but then I remembered police found bits of her scattered all over—the entire park was her grave. "How about over there?" I pointed left, at a cove of trees.

Mom and I trudged to the trees.

Surrounded by them, we stared. The trees' mightiness dwarfed us. They had nothing in common with the nice plants poet Joyce Kilmer described in his poem "Trees." These assholes slouched. They sneered. They emitted carnivorous desire. My arm hairs prickled.

"Pon lo allí." Mom gestured at the tallest tree's skirt.

Penetrating its canopy, I lifted drooping limbs. I exposed trunk. Tree torso.

I leaned the yellow rose bouquet I'd forgotten was tucked under my arm against the gray bark. This was what we'd come here to do. To abandon dead plants with living ones.

I eyeballed my tribute, waiting for relief to wash away my shitty feelings, but my offering suddenly seemed insignificant. Dumb, in fact. The breeze whisked the cellophane wrapper, crinkling it. Its orange price tag made me feel cheap. "I'm gonna take off the price tag," I said. I knelt and clawed at it, peeling it away.

Behind the trees, chubby Mexican girls, versions of me forever ago, sprinted across playground sand. They panted prediabetically. They had cheeks to feed families with.

I wondered which little girl would steal the flowers once we left. I figured one of them would get the idea to use them as a prop in the not-quite-rapeish game of You're Gonna Marry Me. When I was those little girls' age, I'd excelled at You're Gonna Marry Me liztaylorishly. My size facilitated my polygamy. Skinny fuckers had to accept my proposals or I'd sit on them.

The damp grass was making my knees prune, so I got up. I turned. Mom turned with me. We stared at the baseball diamond. We stared at the elementary school behind it.

I wondered, "How do you beat someone to death feet away from where children will be eating paste in a few hours?"

Little Leaguers were jogging the bases. Their cleats kicked up puffs of dirt. Their coach yelled something indecipherable at them. Good coaches speak in tongues. They're Pentecostal.

The ghost I brought the flowers for appeared on the flat pitcher's mound. In the long dark skirt the news said she was wearing the night she died, she began running toward home.

Through the snack bar window, I glimpsed a man in a white jersey. He reached for a stereo sitting next to a bag of chips on the counter and cranked up the volume. The lyric "How far is heaven?" chorused.

The whole neighborhood heard the question. Even Dad heard it.

// //

As he pulled away from the curb, Dad pointed at the grass.

"That's where the baseball bleachers used to be," he said. "The city took them out because homeless people were sleeping underneath."

I imagined her beneath them, smashed like a cucaracha.

"I think they moved them for other reasons," I said.

We cruised up the street and past tract homes with cluttered yards, shabby chicanismo. Sparrows bathed in a gothic birdbath. Christmas lights ringed a particleboard doghouse. A row of toilets lined a driveway. Piles of stuffed animals rotted beside a slumped porch. A blond Virgin Mary statue stared down a racially ambiguous one across the street. A plaster stag, doe, and fawn prettied crabgrass. A fading Lakers banner draped a hibiscus tree. A rusty flagpole waved the Mexican flag.

"Huh," said Dad. "I didn't know the Mexican consulate was here."

A brunette Virgin statue, a decapitated Virgin statue, a concrete Virgin with fresh-cut cacti at her feet, a Virgin weeping blood, a Virgin wearing a Raiders jersey.

"I remember when white people used to live here," said Dad.

"There were no virgins in the yards then, huh?" I added rhetorically.

// //

Dad parked in front of Super Food Co Max. He buzzed down the car windows. He and Mom left us.

My girlfriend and I panted in the backseat. I felt like a dog. I said, "Tell me the story about your grandpa putting you in the dog cage." She obliged, describing how her grandfather would babysit her and lock her in a kennel so she'd be safe while he drank whisky.

// //

Dad was back. He passed me a bag full of pastrami. I set it by my feet. He started the engine.

"Yo quiero Taco Bell!" said Mom.

"Yo también!" said Dad. To my girlfriend, he said, "That means *me too.*"

"Thank you," she said with almost undetectable sarcasm. White people are *so good* at modulating sarcasm. They do it so well you almost don't notice it.

// //

Sitting in Taco Bell, I thought about how in my head, at the park, while glancing up at the clouds puffing innocent shapes in the sky, I had addressed her. I had addressed the ghost who'd haunted me for more than a decade. "I'm not glad you're dead, but I'm glad I'm alive," I'd told her. "I'm glad I can keep feeling sunlight fade my tattoos. I'm glad I can keep inhaling the corticosteroid nasal spray that relieves my allergy symptoms. I'm glad I can keep on listening to right-wing talk radio for fun."

I bowed my head at the chalupa on the tray before me. In the context of our morning pilgrimage, it assumed the status of holy object. Relic. I peeled off its paper wrapper.

My fingers parted its doughy lips. Sealed by sour cream, they made that noise some girls make when you open them.

A woman was sacrificed so that I might sit here, autopsying my chalupa.

I noticed body parts floating inside the gooey rice: two coarse strands of hair.

I was alive and she was dead, so I ate. I ate my lunch, hair and all. We are all cannibals.

Radio

She still doesn't leave me alone. She's still here. And it's still mostly through the radio that she makes her presence known. I'll linger on a station I can't stand and wonder, "Why am I listening to this?" Then I'll realize: *she's listening to this.*

She enjoys music through me. She enjoys food through me. She enjoys sunsets through me. She enjoys the smell of certain flowers through me. It's OK for ghosts to exist through me. It has to be.

// //

Somewhere out there, Ida is probably smoking crack on accident. And a woman is getting touched to death.

Coffee House Press began as a small letterpress operation in 1972 and has grown into an internationally renowned nonprofit publisher of literary fiction, essay, poetry, and other work that doesn't fit neatly into genre categories.

Coffee House is both a publisher and an arts organization. Through our *Books in Action* program and publications, we've become interdisciplinary collaborators and incubators for new work and audience experiences. Our vision for the future is one where a publisher is a catalyst and connector.

LITERATURE
is not the same thing as
PUBLISHING

Emily Books is a publishing project that champions transgressive, genre-blurring writing by (mostly) women. Its founders are Ruth Curry and Emily Gould.

Funder Acknowledgments

Coffee House Press is an internationally renowned independent book publisher and arts nonprofit based in Minneapolis, MN; through its literary publications and *Books in Action* program, Coffee House acts as a catalyst and connector—between authors and readers, ideas and resources, creativity and community, inspiration and action.

Coffee House Press books are made possible through the generous support of grants and donations from corporations, state and federal grant programs, family foundations, and the many individuals who believe in the transformational power of literature. This activity is made possible by the voters of Minnesota through a Minnesota State Arts Board Operating Support grant, thanks to the legislative appropriation from the arts and cultural heritage fund. Coffee House also receives major operating support from the Amazon Literary Partnership, the Jerome Foundation, The McKnight Foundation, Target Foundation, and the National Endowment for the Arts (NEA). To find out more about how NEA grants impact individuals and communities, visit www.arts.gov.

Coffee House Press receives additional support from the Elmer L. & Eleanor J. Andersen Foundation; the David & Mary Anderson Family Foundation; the Buuck Family Foundation; Dorsey & Whitney LLP; Fredrikson & Byron, P.A.; the Fringe Foundation; Kenneth Koch Literary Estate; the Knight Foundation; the Rehael Fund of the Minneapolis Foundation; the Matching Grant Program Fund of the Minneapolis Foundation; Mr. Pancks' Fund in memory of Graham Kimpton; the Schwab Charitable Fund; Schwegman, Lundberg & Woessner, P.A.; the U.S. Bank Foundation; VSA Minnesota for the Metropolitan Regional Arts Council; and the Woessner Freeman Family Foundation in honor of Allan Kornblum.

The Publisher's Circle of Coffee House Press

Publisher's Circle members make significant contributions to Coffee House Press's annual giving campaign. Understanding that a strong financial base is necessary for the press to meet the challenges and opportunities that arise each year, this group plays a crucial part in the success of Coffee House's mission.

Recent Publisher's Circle members include many anonymous donors, Suzanne Allen, Patricia A. Beithon, Bill Berkson & Connie Lewallen, E. Thomas Binger & Rebecca Rand Fund of the Minneapolis Foundation, Robert & Gail Buuck, Claire Casey, Louise Copeland, Jane Dalrymple-Hollo, Ruth Stricker Dayton, Jennifer Kwon Dobbs & Stefan Liess, Mary Ebert & Paul Stembler, Chris Fischbach & Katie Dublinski, Kaywin Feldman & Jim Lutz, Sally French, Jocelyn Hale & Glenn Miller, the Rehael Fund-Roger Hale/Nor Hall of the Minneapolis Foundation, Randy Hartten & Ron Lotz, Dylan Hicks & Nina Hale, Jeffrey Hom, Carl & Heidi Horsch, Amy L. Hubbard & Geoffrey J. Kehoe Fund, Kenneth Kahn & Susan Dicker, Stephen & Isabel Keating, Kenneth Koch Literary Estate, Allan & Cinda Kornblum, Leslie Larson Maheras, Lenfestey Family Foundation, Sarah Lutman & Rob Rudolph, the Carol & Aaron Mack Charitable Fund of the Minneapolis Foundation, George & Olga Mack, Joshua Mack & Ron Warren, Gillian McCain, Mary & Malcolm McDermid, Sjur Midness & Briar Andresen, Maureen Millea Smith & Daniel Smith, Peter Nelson & Jennifer Swenson, Marc Porter & James Hennessy, Enrique Olivarez, Jr. & Jennifer Komar, Alan Polsky, Robin Preble, Jeffrey Scherer, Jeffrey Sugerman & Sarah Schultz, Alexis Scott, Nan G. & Stephen C. Swid, Patricia Tilton, Stu Wilson & Melissa Barker, Warren D. Woessner & Iris C. Freeman, Margaret Wurtele, Joanne Von Blon, and Wayne P. Zink & Christopher Schout.

For more information about the Publisher's Circle and other ways to support Coffee House Press books, authors, and activities, please visit www.coffeehousepress.org/support or contact us at info@coffeehousepress.org.

Myriam Gurba lives in California and loves it. She teaches high school, writes, and makes "art." NBC described her short story collection *Painting Their Portraits in Winter* as "edgy, thought-provoking, and funny." She has written for *Time,* KCET, and the *Rumpus.* Wildflowers, compliments, and cash make her happy.